Leaders praise *Destination Success* for bringing you practical coaching results

"*Destination Success* is a fresh approach to balancing your life using humor, stories, and practical exercises to overcome obstacles that handicap us from our dreams."

> **Mark Victor Hansen**, co-creator, #1 *New York Times* bestselling series Chicken Soup for the Soul®; co-author, *The One Minute Millionaire*

"Dwight Bain is one of the most encouraging men I know. Just being around him makes me feel that I can be better and live higher. Thousands have been motivated by listening to him teach. Now a book . . . and it should be no surprise that *Destination Success* reflects the power and enthusiasm of the writer. Read this book. You'll thank me for recommending it to you."

> **Steve Brown**, bestselling author and host of Key Life Radio Network

"*Destination Success* is truly destined to be one of the classics in achieving success in life. My friend Dwight Bain writes in a clear, precise, and compelling fashion, and when you're finished reading this book your life will never be the same."

> **Pat Williams**, bestselling author; senior VP, The Orlando Magic

"In *Destination Success*, Dwight Bain shows how you can live your dreams even when life's unsuspected blows bring great setbacks. Dwight's keen insights set you on a course for success."

Steve Arterburn, bestselling author; founder of New Life Clinics & Women of Faith conferences

"In athletics, the best coaches are often those who previously succeeded as players by understanding, mastering, and applying the game's fundamentals. They were the player who made his teammates better. Dwight has played the game and in *Destination Success* he shows you how to win. His practical, achievable strategies for success will get you going in the right direction."

Bob Ban de Pol, PhD, president of Crisis Care Network

"Perhaps the most impressive thing about *Destination Success* was the climactic ending. He built a solid case for success as a journey throughout the twelve chapters and topped it off perfectly at the conclusion. Success not only as a journey but also as a process is another strong theme of the book. I strongly recommend this book to success seekers. It will feed your soul with good nutrition."

Dr. W. G. Covington Jr., Amazon.com Top 1000 Reviewer

DESTINATION
SUCCESS

DESTINATION
SUCCESS

FOREWORD BY
JOHN C. MAXWELL

DWIGHT BAIN

© 2003 by Dwight Bain

Published by Revell
a division of Baker Publishing Group
P.O. Box 6287, Grand Rapids, MI 49516-6287
www.revellbooks.com

Spire edition published 2009
ISBN 978-0-8007-8788-2

Printed in the United States of America

Unless otherwise indicated, Scripture is taken from the HOLY BIBLE, NEW IN-
TERNATIONAL VERSION®. NIV®. Copyright © 1973, 1978, 1984 by International Bible Society. Used by permission of Zondervan. All rights reserved.

Scripture marked KJV is taken from the King James Version of the Bible.

Scripture marked NKJV is taken from the New King James Version. Copyright ©
1982 by Thomas Nelson, Inc. Used by permission. All rights reserved.

Scripture marked TLB is taken from *The Living Bible*, copyright © 1971. Used by
permission of Tyndale House Publishers, Inc., Wheaton, IL 60189. All rights
reserved.

09   10   11   12   13   14   15   7   6   5   4   3   2   1

To Clint and May Bain,
my dear Mom and Dad

You taught me about lasting success;
then you showed me the way.
I am forever grateful.

I honor you by teaching
and showing others.

I love you both and am so
grateful that we are friends.

Contents

Foreword by John C. Maxwell 11

Introduction 15

Part 1   The Success Focus

1. Secret #1: Defining What Success Means to You 25
2. Envisioning Success 44
3. Secret #2: Finding Success Every Day 64
4. What to Do with the Elvis in You 79

Part 2   The Success Fear

5. Facing Your Success Fears 99
6. Secret #3: Building Success by Mastering Yourself 117
7. Self-Sabotage—The Most Dangerous Part of You 135
8. Secret #4: Developing Personal Discipline to Discover Your Destiny 153

Contents

Part 3 The Success Formula

9. Secret #5: Belief—Finding Your Hidden Source of Inner Strength 175
10. Secret #6: Opportunity—Discovering Your Success Magnet 194
11. Secret #7: Excellence—Living the Life You've Always Wanted 211
12. Success Seekers Keep Climbing 227

Notes 247
Acknowledgments 249

FOREWORD

Several years ago I challenged my friend Dwight Bain to write this book. After discussing leadership and team-building principles with him, I knew that his insights would be helpful to many people on their personal journey of success.

For thirty years I have taught people that success is not a one-time destination, but rather a lifetime journey. You will never get to that place where you finally "have it all" and no longer need to reach further. But each day you have the choice to continue growing and developing into the type of person you were designed to be, living at a new level. In this book, Dwight will act as your personal success coach to carefully guide you and lead you on a new path as you begin to live out your dreams.

I first met Dwight in Denver during a radio interview that was supposed to last for only ten minutes but went on until we ran out of tape! I discovered that Dwight was a creative and fun communicator, and we became friends as I mentored him in leadership. Then a wonderful thing happened. Dwight began sharing insights and illustrations with me from his own research, which he uses for radio, television, and personal speaking engagements. Each week he sends me a fax or email with new quotes and stories. As a writer, speaker, and business owner, I have benefited from his eye for great stories and wonderful illustrations that are easy to apply to daily living.

Dwight has an amazing ability to quickly assimilate ideas from the many experts he has interviewed and from the nuggets of wisdom he has gained from coaching and counseling thousands of people over the last twenty years. Your personal success journey will be enriched and strengthened as you learn and master the seven secrets of success Dwight shares in this book. They are a result of the years he has spent talking to leaders from around the world.

Recently Dwight was in Atlanta with me, and we spoke to a group of leadership coaches. During one of the sessions, Dwight shared an exciting concept from this book, the "Successful Life Formula." It is designed to help you instantly know where you are and what you need to be working on to experience the quality of life you desire. I could feel the excitement in the room as the audience began to discover their own areas of strength and weakness within just a few minutes. From this exercise they were able to identify exactly which areas they needed to develop in order to focus on living at a new level of success. Dwight's success formula can also help you to discover where you are in contrast with where you want to be on your own success journey.

I know that Dwight can lead you to a new level, one that includes a balanced and healthier way of living. You will learn how to overcome your success fears, find the success that is available to you right now, and be encouraged to continue on toward a life of lasting success. I look forward to hearing about your successes as you begin to live out your dreams.

All the best to you as you uncover the secrets to a better way of life!

John C. Maxwell, Founder
The Injoy Group
Atlanta

Introduction

Have you ever wondered why you aren't more successful? Have you had the same thought about a business associate, friend, or family member who seems to have much potential yet is never really successful at anything? I sure have, and I have seen some amazing contrasts. People with virtually no ability to become successful have seemingly done the impossible, while others who appear to be loaded with looks, money, and talent never seem to get it together. They look like they have it all yet never really experience lasting success.

Are You as Successful as You Want to Be?

I have studied the lives of thousands of people over the last two decades as a success coach and counselor. I saw two remarkable distinctions between those who were really living the life they wanted and others who never quite reached their dreams. One group, a very small group, always seemed to win in spite of the odds. They had mastered what I came to view as "success secrets." A much larger group seemingly had an *L* imprinted on their foreheads as though they were destined to lose. It seemed they were programmed to fail at everything and never achieve lasting success. I have heard hundreds of excuses from this *L* group. Listen to some recent explanations about why these people never "made it," and see if any of these apply to you or the people in your world.

"I just wasn't smart enough."

"When our business failed, it was over for us."

"I married the wrong woman, and she ruined my life."

"It was the alcohol. One day it just took over."

"My sister got all the breaks. Mom liked her more than me."

"It was my weight, and no one will give a fat person a chance."

"I was always at the wrong place at the wrong time."

"I screwed up my life in college and just never got over it."

"I just never had a chance to be successful."

"I guess I'm just not lucky."

Do you hear the common theme in these explanations about failure in life? Notice the feelings of being totally out of control. Listen to the blame shifting, the avoidance, the escapism as well as the pity. It's no wonder people who think and talk this way fail. There are several reasons people hide behind excuses to explain their lack of success in life.

They tell lies to cover up their failures instead of facing them.

They failed so many times that it hurts to even think about trying again.

They never think about the real issues causing their empty life.

They are asleep, unconscious of the fact that life is going on around them.

They are in serious denial about what is missing in their life.

They never had a coach or mentor to guide them onto a path of success.

They gave up on a better life.

I suspect that it may be a little bit of each of these, yet I discovered some tremendous insights from working with thousands of people overcoming serious difficulties. Problems, pressure, and panic caused one group to give up on their dreams of success while serving as hidden sources of energy for the successful to live out their dreams. I saw the group with the "secrets of success" crash through the very roadblocks that limited or handicapped others. Those who knew the secrets had a significantly better quality of life.

What about you? Are you in the small group who live out their dreams and experience success after success, or is your life checkered by failure after failure? Once you answer that question, here's another.

Do You Get Stronger during Difficult Times?

In the lives I studied, I noticed that some people faced difficult situations and got weaker, which seemed normal until

I noticed others going through identical circumstances who toughened up to become amazingly successful. They lived at a higher level. It was almost as if the problems and stress gave them a shot of turbo-charged fuel to move up to a higher level. When people mastered these secrets, they too had this hidden source of power to live out the life they wanted. Their age, education, or socioeconomic class didn't matter. And their past didn't matter as much as the personal realization that they could live out their hopes and dreams. So consider this question.

Could This Be Your Time to Discover Lasting Success?

I enjoy seeing people come alive when they discover and apply the secrets of success. I love it when coaching clients "get it," when the lightbulb in their mind illuminates with the insight of how to be successful instead of having to face one more crisis, one more failure, one more loss, or one more breakdown. It is always an adventure, and sometimes the most unlikely are the very ones who grasp the secrets of success, apply them, and achieve a quality of life that surprises everyone—everyone but them, that is. Where did they find the fountain of wisdom that allows them to have the unshakable confidence to accomplish their dreams when the majority of people around them seem to be failing?

If you take an honest look at your own life, you will likely see a common pattern in your behavior. The same principle is true of your personal or professional life or of the history of your business, friends, or family. Track the events over time, and it will appear as if there was a mental radar that led straight to another failed relationship, business venture, or personal crisis. Even if your best friend got in your face and begged you to stop, you may have gone over the edge one more time. Like a movie script that predicted a series of breakdowns and failures, you fell down right on cue.

Isn't It Time to Rewrite the Script?

So how can you undo the dangerous flaws that set you up to fail and reverse the process to set yourself up to win? Simple: You have to master the seven secrets of success, the essential beliefs and behaviors practiced by the most successful people in our culture. These elements are usually overlooked and rarely used, which is why I call them secrets. When uncovered and practiced, however, these secrets lead to a significantly better quality of life. Since you and I know that you need to make some radical changes to experience lasting success, let's get started in the direction of your dreams. Our new destination: success! Let's take action to experience the quality of life you have always wanted to live. Let's work together to rewrite the script of your life to include lasting success this time around.

I am going to serve as your personal success coach to guide you past the subtle dangers that have been stealing your creative ability to think successfully. Together we will discover and disarm other dangers that have either blocked or seemingly eliminated the incredible things available to you. If you will allow me, I can lead you onto the pathway of success that you have been missing. If not, you may be stuck on a dead-end road without a plan and doomed to miss out on the life that you could have experienced. It's time to choose what kind of life you are going to have. I believe it's time for you to choose success.

This book will get you moving toward a more successful way of living. We will journey through seven secrets and arrive at the final destination, becoming a "success seeker," a person who has mastered the seven secrets. A success seeker has learned how to find success every day and gone on to share it with others. The map outlined in *Destination Success* will guide you into living at a higher level, experiencing a better life than you previously imagined. As we partner together, I will challenge your thinking, especially on what lasting success means. Our goal is to achieve positive results in the areas of life that matter most to you.

The first part of our journey together is to discover more success in your life. I call the secrets contained in this part of our trip the "success focus." We will flesh out a clear definition of what success looks like to you at this stage of life. These secrets will help you avoid spending your time and energy on activities that don't move you toward the quality of life you desire. If your goal is to feel successful every day, you must master the ability to find success. Learning these secrets will help you do that.

Then we will partner together to discover success you thought was lost. This is the second part of *Destination Success*, where we will face and disarm your success fear. This area is the biggest roadblock to fulfillment of one's dreams. The secrets in this section will guide you away from repeating a self-destructive pattern of behavior in your personal life or business. This is the most exciting part for me, because I will teach you how to stretch your old roadblocks into a new shape to become the bridge to a new level of success. Think of it! We are going to move beyond the mistakes to a new level of accomplishment in your business, finances, and personal relationships.

Most important is the third aspect, the "success formula," where we will build some daily routines that, when practiced, will allow you to live out more success every single day. I have seen this formula work for thousands of people, and it will work for you as well. When you remove the roadblocks to success, you won't find this formula difficult to apply. As you live out the seven secrets, you will not only be better equipped for success, you will begin to experience the quality of life that only success seekers experience. The good news is that the path is open and available to anyone who will take the journey to arrive at a destination called "success"!

Are you ready to move toward success?

Then let's go!

PART I

THE SUCCESS FOCUS

To laugh often and much;
To win the respect of intelligent people
    and the affection of children,
To earn the appreciation of honest critics
    and endure the betrayal of false friends;
To appreciate beauty,
To find the best in others,
To leave the world a bit better
    whether by a healthy child, a garden patch,
    or a redeemed social condition;
To know even one life has breathed easier
    because you lived.
This is to have succeeded.

              —Ralph Waldo Emerson

ONE

Secret #1

DEFINING WHAT SUCCESS MEANS TO YOU

Success is a science. If you have the conditions, you get the results.

—Oscar Wilde

Fool's gold is not what it seems. Many people seeking their fortune in the Old West were thrown off by the iron ore that glittered but wasn't gold. They couldn't spend it, because it was worthless. Many people have a concept of success that is like fool's gold. They falsely believe that if you look successful, you are successful. I call that image management. They dress up, put on a happy face, and say, "I'm fine. I'm just great!" Instead of actually looking at their life and measuring what is most valuable, they adopt the philosophy of "fake it till you make it." The problem is that they don't know what "make it" is. Somewhere along the line they came to believe that success is simply "having it all." While their lives may look like they have it all together both personally and professionally, what looks successful on the outside really isn't. The saying "All that glitters is not gold" came from people who thought they had struck it rich when they found a bunch of shiny rocks. Likewise, our lives aren't successful because of glitter.

Have you ever felt the pressure to work on the outside of the "package" instead of on the real and valuable gifts inside? It's sort of like the bumper sticker that says, "You Can Never Be Too Rich or Too Thin," implying that more wealth or extreme weight loss is the definition of success. While those things may be important, there is much more to success than the package. Picture it: You are exchanging gifts with a friend, and he or she hands you a beautiful, shiny jewelry box. Your hand trembles as you open it, only to discover that it is full of rocks; it is just a glittering box of rocks. That is like some people: They look successful on the outside but feel worthless on the inside. That's not success.

I once saw in the weather department of a television station a sign that said, "We have two classes of forecasters: those who don't know and those who don't know they don't know." I suspect the same rule applies to success. A few people intuitively know they have some learning, growing, and developing to do, while the other group moves forward with a false sense of confidence because they have the "look." They have the right clothes, right body size, right car, right house, right jewelry, right cologne, right friends, right job, right pet, even the right toothpaste! Deep down inside though, they know they're a sham. They feel the extreme emptiness of a beautiful shell of a life that is really going nowhere.

The beaches of the barrier islands off the southwest coast of Florida illustrate this. Sanibel, Captiva, and Marco islands are nestled in the Gulf of Mexico and have some of the most exotic shells imaginable, with a few tropical species that cannot be found anywhere else in the world. Often the shells can be found in huge mounds several feet thick. They are beautiful shells with vibrant colors and amazing shapes, but when you find them on the beach, they aren't living anymore. The previous occupants stopped growing, died, and washed up on shore. Their life is over, and they are only good for children to collect in sand buckets for decorations or craft projects. It is against federal law to take a living shell from the ocean environment, because living shells keep growing and moving, and they never wash up! You can take as many dead shells as you like, because they are worthless. Think about that again: *The living ones keep growing and never wash up!*

What about you? Do you feel washed up? Do you feel like an empty, lifeless shell? Are you just waiting for someone to pick you up and solve your problems?

If any of these questions stirred your thinking, good! On this journey toward our destination of a successful life, you will find areas of your life that are not growing at all. You also will discover some stable areas and likely some areas that are totally out of control that need immediate attention. The introspection of what is causing you to miss out on greater success may be uncomfortable at times, but honestly looking at your strengths and weaknesses is a vital part of gaining a healthy lifestyle. Mark Twain said, "The truth will set you free, but first it will make you miserable." So get ready to feel miserable and then to feel great as you begin to live out a better life. We will tackle some huge problems that have been holding you back from success, but don't panic. Just be honest about where you are, and then begin to set new goals toward successful life destinations.

Finding Success in Strange Places

Henry Ford once said, "You cannot build a reputation on what you are going to do." Stories could be told of countless people who looked successful but never accomplished anything, while others whom you and I would have labeled with a big *L* for loser changed their corner of the world. Success isn't always what it seems.

One of the best examples of this is the early failure and then incredible success of William Sydney Porter. Unless you paid attention in college English classes, you don't know that name, so let me refresh your memory. He went to the Ohio state penitentiary for embezzlement, where he wrote fourteen stories in his prison cell. He is one of America's favorite authors because of his powerful use of surprise endings mingled with a tremendous sense of human emotion. He wrote stories like "The Last Leaf," "The Ransom of Red Chief," and "The Gift of the Magi," which firmly established him as a gifted storyteller. He wrote under the pen name of O. Henry, and when released from prison in 1901, he was one of the most sought-after writers of his day. He made bad decisions early in life, and one might have labeled him a loser because he was a convicted felon. But that judgment would have been wrong, for Porter has become known worldwide as one of the best short-story writers ever. Be careful that you don't judge success by what people look like, what they have done, or by mistakes they have made. Success is sometimes hard to spot at first glance. Besides, it's not a first glance that matters with success, just like it's not the glitter that makes gold valuable. Gold is valuable because it's gold. The purity of what's on the inside is the only thing that matters for gold or for successful people.

I noticed this truth in the life of singer and actress Bette Midler during her "Divine Miss M" tour. She said in interviews that during her childhood she became inspired to go into music but for the wrong reasons. She now shows tremendous insight on what matters most in life, but admits that she began by chasing the "glitter" of success. Most people want success more than anything. Some people would give up everything, perhaps even their life, to look successful. The irony is that they might do anything to be known as a success before they even know what success is! The humorist Erma Bombeck described this by saying, "Don't confuse fame with success. Madonna is one; Helen Keller is the other." Bette's career evolved from singer to actress to superstar. She displayed more passion and peace with each movie role and album. She got involved in her community. Part of that may be the wisdom that comes from age or the emptiness that comes from "having it all" and wondering if "that's all there is" to life. Her insight shows the difference between people who talk about success and those who live it.

One of the most common yet dangerous approaches to success is to ignore it, or worse, just believe that it will show up one day. Life is not a fairy tale, and success does not just happen. If you leave your life on autopilot, you are likely to crash. The Success Focus begins when you learn to spend your energy and attention on *becoming* successful instead of just *looking* successful. No one respects a wanna-be. The Success Focus is about changing one's focus from appearances to attitudes, from buying beautiful things to being a beautiful person, from joining a health club to actually working out, from picking up a bestselling book to reading it, from talking about a better life to taking bold steps to actually go out and live it.

What about you? Do you feel successful? What does the word *success* really mean? More important, what does it mean to you?

I asked more than a hundred people what success meant to them. Here are some of their rather candid answers. As you read through them, think about how you would define success.

Achieving my goals.

Money.

Being in a loving relationship.

Getting my emotional needs met.

Going for a long walk.

Good health.

Great family and friends.

Having the right house, right car, right husband, and being a perfect size 6.

Being comfortable after a good night's sleep.

Playing golf as much as possible.

Being where you want to be professionally.

Feeling close to God at worship services.

Being well balanced and peaceful.

Getting taken up with another in conversation and losing track of time.

Becoming an executive VP with financial security.

Passing my business along to my grandchildren.

Traveling to exotic places on someone else's credit card.

Visiting the Holy Land.

Jogging, when my mind clears and things come into perspective.

It's available to everyone except me.

Success is a personal feeling; it's being happy and complete.

It's an attitude.

I don't know what it is, but I know that I want it!

That last one was from a guy sitting in the next barber chair while I was getting my hair cut. It made me laugh until I realized he was serious! Sadly, his answer was one of the most common I heard. This exercise quickly revealed a person's values, so I asked different people with whom I have worked in media through the years and came up with more thoughtful responses.

Central Florida's most popular morning deejay, Lisa Williams of Z 88.3 FM and Zradio.org, said that success is "figuring out God's will for my life and then just doing it." Her spiritual values shaped her concept of success.

Inc magazine's 1994 entrepreneur of the year and founder of New Life Clinics, Steve Arterburn, said that success is "a stable family and financial solvency." Notice the balance of his personal values of relationships and business profitability.

Dr. Jeff Gardere, radio and television personality in New York City, said, "Success is not based on money and possessions, but rather on possessing the character to achieve through tenacity, honesty, fair play, and spirituality." Dr. Jeff focused on character development instead of popularity. He believes a healthy soul defines a successful life.

Health and fitness expert Joe Christiano said, "Success is like a walk in an orchard you've tended for years where the fruit is finally ready for others!" Joe discovered a body-redesigning formula for Hollywood celebrities and envisioned developing and distributing those successful secrets to help others find stronger bodies and minds. Sharing health was his way of defining success.

Pat Williams of the Orlando Magic told me, "The best definition of success I've ever heard comes from John Wooden. I can't improve on it: 'Success is peace of mind, which is a direct result of self-satisfaction in knowing you did your best every day to become the best that you are capable of becoming.'" He knows that NBA superstars have to push themselves to reach their potential, and so do you.

Ruth Williams is Pat's wife and a Franklin Covey consultant and coach. She had a specific message for women. "The successful woman is the average woman—focused. That's the key—focus." She knows that a crystal clear view of success helps anyone to find it sooner.

Emmy-winning TV lighting designer Tony Digrolomo said, "Success is getting up every day and doing the things that I hope will please God, and at the end of the battle for that day, prayer, a restful night, and again, here comes the sun . . . success has begun." His belief system motivated him to become excellent in his industry.

National medical media expert Dr. Walt Larimore said, "The good things in life—right marriage, right job, right kids, right amount of money, right car or house or clothes, etc., can only be added to the most important element of wellness—seeking and knowing our Creator. If we believe in and trust God, if we first seek him, if he controls and empowers our lives, then this will always result in wholeness at the deepest level of our being." Walt equates lasting success with the peace that comes from living out a personal faith in God.

There are as many definitions of success as there are people, so what about your definition? Imagine that you and I are on an Indiana Jones type of adventure. You will need seven keys to open the greatest treasure of a lifetime. You will pick up these seven secret keys through seven challenging stages of the adventure leading to a great destination—success! Each success secret will be the key to the treasure trove of your dreams, because when mastered, they will give you the life you have always wanted, the successful life you were designed to live. Ready? Here's the first secret key on our journey toward lasting success.

 The first success secret is to define what success means to you.

It is absolutely critical to have a personal definition of success if you want to achieve it. You must have a clear mental picture of what you want to accomplish before you can move forward to do it. You must see it vividly, because clarity in the image creates motivation and energy to move toward success. This is a basic principle in goal-setting that applies to every aspect of life. Philosopher George Santayana said it this way: "Knowledge of what is possible is the beginning of success."

Can you picture what the word *success* means in different areas of life? Can you look back in your life and see successful times? Perhaps it was when you broke a business profitability record or when you planned a trip and spent it with close friends. Maybe it was when you achieved a healthy level of physical fitness. Perhaps it was a time when you felt loving closeness and connection in a relationship. Maybe it was when you completed a college course while parenting a couple of kids. Or it might be the feeling you have of being connected to God in a peaceful and serene way.

As you can tell, success is a fluid concept. It moves. It changes. It is vibrant, alive, wonderful, and real. And, oh yes, success is available to you! My mentor John Maxwell says, "Success is a continuing thing. It is growth and development. It is achieving one thing and using that as a stepping-stone to achieve something else." Every event in life can lead to more success. Your failures, mistakes, and problems can become the pathway to greater strength. After watching thousands of people rebuild their lives, I know that success doesn't come naturally. If anything, the propensity to fail is natural. Our mental autopilot tends toward avoiding painful things, so moving forward to reach greater success will be a tough challenge at times. It will be hard work.

Danger: Watch Out!

Aggressively avoid the tendency to think that life will just "fall into place" for you if you do nothing. Life may fall on you, but you probably won't like the results! Life often places us in situations we are not prepared for, that we think we should know more about and therefore can handle. The consequences for failing are remarkably painful. They include such things as bankruptcy, divorce, heart attack, eviction, jail time, foreclosure, and death. Be alert. This is not a game. There are no "push the reset button and try again" options. If you end up crashing, you will hurt yourself and others. You won't get a second chance at life.

Your definition of success will impact you in a profound way and will ripple into every other aspect of life as well. Consider these elements of success:

- If you achieve financial success, you can bless the lives of your family, friends, and those in your community through charitable work.
- If you achieve physical success, you may outlive the impact of self-imposed health problems from obesity or lung, liver, or heart disease. As you live longer and healthier, you can enjoy the feeling of connection with your family and friends doing things you really enjoy instead of slipping off into oblivion on a couch with a

remote control in one hand and a bowl of chips in the other.

- If you experience spiritual success, you will feel a sense of purpose and peace that you are living according to your deepest values and convictions, which gives an incredible sense of meaning as you live out your mission.

- If you build and develop relationship success, you will find a deep and lasting sense of comfort as you connect in heart and soul to the people who matter the most to you.

- If you find success in your career, you will look forward to every day with a "T.G.I.T." mentality—"Thank God It's Today!" Then Monday will become your most exciting day of the week, because it means that you can go back to doing the things you love to do and get paid to do them!

- As you discover emotional success, you will feel a sense of peace about who you are and will gain mastery over your moods. You will be happier with yourself and be less preoccupied with living the "fake it till you make it" philosophy. People who try to fake their way through life never really enjoy anything and usually end up crashing instead of arriving at a successful destination.

How Do You Define Success?

Have you begun to seriously think about your definition of success? If not, don't panic. The Success Focus is about fleshing out what success means to you. It will require some time and thought, and I will guide you through the process step by step.

One of the joys of coaching people is listening to the remarkable insights that emerge when they take out a pen and legal pad to focus on what success means. Here are a couple of recent examples from leaders I coached through the process of this first secret. See if their definitions are helpful as you begin to develop your own concept of success.

John Bruneau is a successful businessman in a great marriage with his wife, Sharon. He has a detailed view of success that "filters" every decision he makes.

Success is a personal feeling. It is a combination of being happy and "complete." The feelings of being complete come from having fulfilling personal experiences.

Others cannot deem you a success. You will not ultimately feel successful just because others look at you as successful or call you a success. These are nice compliments that can make you feel good temporarily, but what others think or say cannot make you feel fulfilled or complete.

Material things (cars, homes, jewelry, stereos, etc.) can produce the following feelings: "I like this" or "This is nice" or even "This feels good." This looks great to others, but these feelings don't "fill" you or make you feel "whole" or "complete." They only make you feel good temporarily. Without feeling whole or complete, you will not feel successful; and you will be left searching for more and more to fill the void. Dining out in nice restaurants or taking elaborate vacation trips may bring about a fulfilling experience (personal connection), but the particular restaurant or vacation destination itself is not the fulfilling experience.

Financial wealth is not an indication of success. There are numerous businessmen, movie stars, musical stars, sports stars, and entertainers who are extremely well off, yet they do not feel complete or whole or at peace with themselves. Only to the extent that money eliminates worry (for instance, making the mortgage payment), can it help contribute to achieving success. The elimination of worry helps remove barriers to having fulfilling experiences.[1]

Notice how John covered several areas in his definition—financial, relational, and career experiences. Notice also that one of the ways he defines success in his own life is by making a contrast with what success doesn't mean to him. John has a vivid picture of what success looks like and a detailed plan to find it. Once you have your success path mapped out, you'll discover significantly more success too.

Here's a definition from Linda Seyer, a successful female executive, who suddenly lost her husband to an aggressive form of cancer. She was rebuilding her world after losing her best friend and was trying to find a new meaning for success when she wrote these words.

Success is a feeling of total contentment and confidence that you are at the pinnacle of your self-scheduled goals for this season of your life.

Success is a reward for hard work and perseverance, for caring so much that you get tunnel vision.

Success has little to do with luck. Success requires patience. Success requires planning. Success is the mastery of techniques to attain the ultimate goal.

Success is a lifelong goal that is elusive to most people. The successful person is revered in our society, adored by the unsuccessful as well as the successful want-to-bes.

Success is born through wisdom, instinct, intuitiveness, experience, and lots of hard work. It is a feeling of a job well done.

Success can be attained in all aspects of a person's life. Some of the most rewarding successes are personal or spiritual in nature and not work related.

A person who equates his success ratio with only work-related issues is not a truly successful person. The only true gauge of success is measured in that person's heart.

Success is a pat on the back, sometimes short lived, as a reward for many long hours and sometimes even years of painstaking effort. The title is usually well deserved and long overdue.

The truly successful person exudes an aura of peace and fulfillment that is coveted by everyone who comes in contact with this extraordinary person. Such persons are our mentors and our heroes. They are well loved.[2]

Wow! Linda listed the emotional concepts of contentment, fulfillment, and spirituality. She had more than just a single focus, which is why she was able to experience peace in the midst of tragedy. Within a few years, she moved, changed jobs, and eventually remarried with this mental picture of rebuilding the life she wanted. Linda's definition of success guided her through some dark and difficult days to a new place of enlightened contentment.

The Courage to Move Beyond Average

Today you may call yourself average. You may have believed until now that you had "tapped out" on your opportunity to experience success. No! Your life is not over! You have been wonderfully designed by God to stretch and grow. You are not simply getting older; with continual personal growth, you can get better. You have probably been to graduations that included a tribute to those special students who were significantly older because they went back to finish a degree at a later stage of life. This is typical at college commencement services of women who put their careers on hold to raise children and then went back to finish college. This is heroic, because it takes a lot of courage to finish something you started twenty years earlier. Let me tell you about one of the most powerful experiences of this type of courage I've seen.

Dave Stanley is a self-taught minister from the mountains of southeastern Kentucky. He had a heart to serve people yet had never finished high school. This is common in the mountains of Appalachia, where people quit school to work and provide for their families. I was speaking at the commencement service where a special tribute to Dave was made because he was receiving his high school diploma. I will never forget how proud everyone was of this middle-aged man who faced his fears to go back and finish high school. He stood on that platform and cried as he accepted the praise and applause of everyone in the building. His courage to boldly finish that degree meant that he had overcome many fears, which made him a greater success in my eyes than any other graduate that night. He was successful because of the obstacles he had overcome to graduate that his teenaged counterparts couldn't even begin to comprehend. When you boldly face your fears and begin to live out a life of success, you will give hope and courage to others as they begin to think about living a better life as well.

Innumerable people would love to hear the applause of their peers as they overcome the obstacles blocking the next "win" in their life. Where do you find that kind of boldness? Author Basil King identified the secret when he said, "Be bold and mighty forces will come to your aid." When you begin to move toward a new successful destination, you will find people, resources, and opportunities along the pathway. As you begin right now to visualize the kind of life you would like to have, think about the events and experiences you would like to see as part of that life. Do they include any of the following?

- to finish a degree
- to complete a marathon
- to start a new business
- to take time with an aged parent in his or her later years

- to have the courage to confront a grandchild's irresponsible behavior
- to make wise investments and watch them grow profitable
- to enjoy a more loving marriage relationship
- to travel and build wonderful family memories
- to do the things that you talk about but never end up doing

If you don't have a clear mental picture of what personal success means, you will find yourself getting lost again and again. Your life may grow into a series of impossible tasks that you cannot accomplish even though you spend countless hours furiously trying to finish them. A frequently quoted Bible verse says, "Where there is no vision, the people perish" (Prov. 29:18 KJV). I believe that a directionless life will likely cause a person to die sooner physically as well as mentally because one's quality of life is gone. Eventually a directionless person may settle for second best or just wear out and give up. Some will wander in silence and become depressed and despondent. Others will be very loud about what they will do "one day," but if you look deep into their eyes, you will see fear and know they never will do what they say—all talk, no action. They will miss the life they could have experienced because they neglected the first secret of success.

What's Your Dream?

Such people remind me of the fast-talking hustler in the opening scene of the 1994 movie *Pretty Woman*. He worked his way through the streets of Southern California, saying, "What's your dream? Everybody in Hollywood's got a dream. So what's your dream?" The movie ends with the same guy still walking the streets. You may recall that the plot involves one couple sorting through the details of their far-fetched relationship and arriving at a fairy-tale ending, while the street hustler just keeps on walking and fast-talking, apparently not any closer to becoming anything significant.

"What's your dream?" is a good question, but without strategically working through the details and using a practical action plan, answering this question is a waste of breath. But if you're ready to live a better quality of life, to begin living as a success seeker, then buckle up; the fun is just about to begin!

Get ready to pick up the seven secrets of a successful life as we move forward on our journey to success. By now you are beginning to think through the different aspects of what success means to you. Good! It may include wealth, influence, power, and business opportunities. It may mean a strong marriage, great kids, and a nice home. Most likely you have added a healthy body and spiritual peace to your success definition. Probably by now you have included the emotional qualities of strong self-worth, confidence, and self-control. Keep thinking about what the word *success* means to you, because it is critically important to living out your dreams. I cannot create the vision of success for you, nor can anyone else. It is already inside you as a gift from God, who programmed an amazing and abundant life into your heart and soul. My job is to help you flesh out what your vision of success is and then show you the pathway to get there sooner than you ever could have imagined.

Are you ready to move toward a successful destination? Then let's get moving toward your dreams!

TWO

ENVISIONING SUCCESS

You see things, and you say "why?"
But I dream things that never were, and say "why not?"

—George Bernard Shaw

A re you living out your dreams? Are you already so successful that most of your days are spent having the time of your life? I hope so, because it would be a tragedy to go through life thinking that you are a failure and that your life is meaningless. To waste even one day feeling moody, unhappy, frustrated, or mad at the world is to waste too much. *Don't do it!* Don't let your life slip away day by day with petty worries and meaningless tasks. If you even have a slight glimpse of a better life, then hold on to it with superglue on both hands. We hear too many tragic stories of men and women who had a shot at a better life but didn't take it. They arrived at the end of life with a sackful of regrets and resentment instead of deep satisfaction over reaching the destination of a life journey that was well spent.

Is Just Being in the Race a Success?

Irony surrounds a line uttered by Marlon Brando in the classic 1954 film *On the Waterfront*: "I coulda had class, I coulda been a contenda instead of a bum." Brando gave such a powerful presentation through the character of Terry Malloy that he won the Oscar for best actor that year. The commercial success of *On the Waterfront* was amazing. It won eight Oscars, including Best Actor, Best Picture, Best Director, and Best Screenplay, making it one of the most successful films of its era. It is interesting that these awards would be given to a movie reflecting one man's struggle to be a "contenda," with his goal in life just to get into the race, let alone win it. Perhaps the story was so well received in our culture because it reflects a struggle all people experience, the struggle to believe that you really can win at life, that you can be a champion instead of just a contender, or worse, only a "bum."

To me it shows that audiences during the stable 1950s were trying to figure out how to do more than their parents, to have a better life for themselves and their children. They were trying to get beyond thinking about the Great Depression and the horrors of World War II that took away any sense of success, since the goal in life was just to hang on and survive. No doubt some people believed that a better life may have been available to people in the movies but not to the average joe on the street. Maybe that's why our culture gravitates toward stories about the underdog who wins against impossible odds. Perhaps it's a reflection of a deep inner belief that common people rarely win. *Not in this lifetime,* you may be thinking. Something in the cosmos is against you and won't ever allow circumstances to favor your success with money, love, health, or career. You shouldn't even think about being successful because it isn't in the cards for you.

Stop Killing Your Creativity!

Stop the self-destructive mentality that kills your creative ability to picture a better life. Begin right now to start thinking like a champion. My clients often struggle as I coach them toward a new pattern of thinking. Maybe you are having the same struggle right now. You may be challenged mentally to see yourself living a better life. Can you see yourself as well balanced, at peace, enjoying each day doing the things you want to do? Can you visualize yourself living well with the people you love, celebrating your blessings, breaking through financial barriers, and having a good time knowing that your best days are still ahead? Can you see yourself waking up every day with the anticipation that today is going to be one more page in a well-lived life story? In the next few pages, I am going to help you understand and master the secret of thinking like a true success, since thinking like a success leads to living like one.

A reporter once asked the great playwright George Bernard Shaw, "Mr. Shaw, you have been wined and dined by all the greats of our generation. They all aspire to your friendship, and you know them well. If you could be reincarnated and come back as some other famous person of our time, who would it be?" Shaw didn't think about it long and replied, "If I could relive my life in the role of any person I desired, I would want to be the man George Bernard Shaw could have been but wasn't." He had accomplished many successful things in his life yet felt that he hadn't lived up to his potential.

Are You Living Your Dreams?

If you sat down right now to answer the question "Are you living out your dreams of success? Are you living out your potential?" what would you write? Would you begin to write furiously and fill up page after page of a legal pad with an exciting life full of joy? Would you write about the places, people, and events that inspire you to wake up every day to see what comes next?

The great major league pitcher Orel Hershiser was asked what his greatest moment in life was. Would it be winning the National League's MVP award, winning the Cy Young Award, pitching in his first World Series, or later winning a world championship and being named MVP of a World Series? Orel had a healthy body, a loving wife, two handsome sons, a beautiful home, great friends, a remarkably successful career in baseball, and a strong Christian faith. What would be his favorite life experience of all? I love his answer: "My greatest moment is the next great moment."

Is that how you would answer? Would you get so carried away with your blessings that you would neglect focusing on the negative things? I have counseled thousands of people through the years and have discovered that many of them hold on to hurts, which makes them miss the joys. They capture a mental image of the worst things that have ever happened to them and block out the blessings. They hold on to pain, problems, and pressure as if that is all they have. Sadly, some people have such empty lives that they think all they have to hold on to are problems, so they hold on with all their might! Before you say that's crazy, think about it for a moment. The human spirit has to hold on to, or believe, in something. It's like a bumper sticker I once saw that said, "Everyone has to believe in something, so I believe I'll have another beer." As odd as that sounds, many people hold on to their negative beliefs and unhealthy behavior instead of holding on to the image of a better life.

A New View of Success

I hope that your life has more pleasure than pain and that you live free from the temptation to embrace problems. I hope that you are able to see yourself in a valuable way, as a winner in life—not necessarily living a perfect life, but definitely a healthy one. As you think about living out your dreams, consider the elements of a fulfilling life. Consider events and emotions like

the trip of a lifetime

enjoying the family ski boat

building a great corporate team

turning a struggling business into a profitable one

spending a full week with your father just to learn from his wisdom completing a half marathon and setting a new personal record

paying off your home mortgage and enjoying being debt free

finishing a tough college class with an A

sleeping until you wake up instead of hearing that pesky alarm

feeling at peace with God and enjoying his presence

losing that last ten pounds and looking great in those jeans

overcoming a problem without "losing it" to a fit of worry or rage

having time to do the things that matter most

donating money to the community organizations you believe in

saying good-bye to your regrets and really feeling good about yourself

feeling loved and valued by those closest to you

This exercise may have been hard for you. Thinking about your life in measurable terms can be pretty scary, especially if you have never mastered the mental process of becoming a success visionary. Everyone likes to talk about success, but many have never sat down to look at what the term actually means. Webster defines success as a noun meaning one of three things: (1) favorable or desired outcome; (2) attainment of wealth, favor, or eminence; (3) one that succeeds.

Think about your life and how successful it is by using this limited definition. If success really means arriving at a favorable outcome, how are you doing? If success means that you feel satisfied with how well you complete tasks, how are you doing? If success means attaining wealth, favor, or eminence, how are you doing? Do you measure up to the dictionary definition, or are you feeling like a loser about now?

To keep a balanced perspective, let's see how Webster defines failure: (1) failing to do or perform; (2) a state of inability to perform a normal function adequately; (3) a lack of success; (4) a falling short, deficiency; (5) deterioration, decay; (6) one that has failed. Failure has twice the number of meanings as success, yet it is easier to define and easier to understand. The dictionary interpretation of success is too limited, too narrow, and too hard to describe. If you measure success in your life by a list of accomplishments and your financial portfolio, you will miss out on many wonderful things. True success is greater than any dictionary could ever define.

The Visionary Process

This chapter will guide you in envisioning your success. You will be able to see it, feel it, and sense it; and most important, you will begin to live out the life you desire. If you can't envision success, you are doomed, because it is the vision of success that will keep you on course during difficult circumstances and help you capture a deep sense of peace and confidence during demanding times. Furthermore, a mental picture of success will create the emotional energy needed to accomplish your dreams. Take out a sheet of paper and answer the following question: "Am I living out my dreams of success?"

If you couldn't fill in anything positive and ended up with a blank sheet of paper entitled "My Life of Extremely Limited Success and Substantial Failure," you are not alone. Jerry Clark, a motivational speaker from Dallas, has found that only 3 percent of the people in his audiences have specific written goals, and even fewer have a targeted plan on how to accomplish them. He typically speaks to highly motivated businesspeople, yet they often don't have a specific plan. Many times they don't have any plan at all! You would hardly go out to the market to buy groceries without a list, much less try to build a successful life without a written plan.

This is very sad news, or very good news, depending on how you look at it. It is sad that so many people miss out on a better way of life by their own failure to flesh out what success means on paper. The good news is that if you can envision a better life, you can change at any time.

Dreamers and Doers

"If you can dream it, you can do it"—that's how Walt Disney described much of what he accomplished. This quote can be found in many places around the theme parks and administrative offices of Disney World in Orlando. It is a powerful thought, because it explains in a single sentence how Disney accomplished so much in such a short span of time. He made movies, theme parks, and television programs that not only impacted his culture but future generations as well.

Think for a minute about how Disney could "see" those movies, theme parks, and television programs in his mind. Was he the only one who could see something before it was built? Of course not. Disney surrounded himself with other gifted, creative people whom he called "imagineers." By Disney's definition, an imagineer is an engineer with vivid imagination. Imagineers are not limited to the way things have always been done. They use the best thinking from the world of science or industry as a launch pad into the uncharted territory of unlimited possibility. They have no ceiling on what can be accomplished. No wonder Disney and his small team changed the face of the entertainment industry forever. Even though they constantly struggled with limited resources of money, time, and staff and often were not accepted by the professional community of their day, they consistently won in the marketplace. You too can be an imagineer as you begin to think outside the lines.

Learn from the Leaders

Read and watch biographical profiles. Study them, learn from them, and listen to the theme of their lives. If you can master the skills of a person who has done something notable, you can save years of time as you model their successful behavior. Think of what you could learn from people like Martin Luther King Jr., Winston Churchill, Bob Hope, Jackie Kennedy Onassis, Ronald Reagan, Oprah Winfrey, Steven Spielberg, Michael Jordan, Bill Cosby, Barbara Bush, or Ted Koppel. Spend time learning from great ones, because there really is truth to the old saying "Birds of a feather flock together." As you study greatness, you will begin to think like a champion and be on your way to living like one.

On the other hand, please don't miss the significance of learning from those who have failed. John Keats said, "Failure is, in a sense, the highway to success, since every discovery of what is false leads us to seek earnestly after what is true." The best way to understand a great person is to see how he or she dealt with failure. I once sat riveted watching a biography of Johnny Cash on VH1. The program showed how he struggled with drugs and alcohol. He went to jail, then made peace with God. And then began the "rocket ride" to the top of his musical career. It was powerful and inspirational to see that he chose a new destination—success! He didn't quit. He beat the odds to come back and win in the very difficult music industry. He held on to his relationships, and he turned his numerous failures into success. You can too. If you watch and listen and learn from the mistakes of great people, you can take a different path to avoid their poor decisions and be years ahead of the game.

Instantly Identify Success

Success is directly linked to your mental picture. I use the following exercise with every client I coach to help identify what success really means. It is one of the fastest ways to become more insightful of what matters most to you so that you can begin to live it out. This exercise will help you to uncover instantly how well you are balanced in the area of success. This is a critical element of your personal growth, so don't rush through it with trite answers. Really think through each of the areas to discover what is or isn't working for you. As you take this profile, answer honestly, as if your closest friends and associates are looking over your shoulder. Lying won't help you achieve success. I sometimes tell clients, "Blowing smoke in your own face will only make you cough." So be honest!

It is best to begin by measuring where you are against your own potential so that you can get an accurate view of your life. Remember, you are measuring yourself in contrast with where you believe you need to be. We are always learning from others, but this exercise isn't about them. It's about you. So clear your mind of comparisons and find a quiet place to complete the following profile.

Bain's Life Success Scale

Date: _____

Take an intense look at your life and score yourself using the following scale to evaluate how successful you believe you are in the major areas of life.

1 = panic	6 = high moderate
2 = extremely weak	7 = low strength
3 = weak	8 = strength
4 = low moderate	9 = high strength
5 = moderate	10 = peak

____ physical health

____ emotional health

____ spiritual health

____ financial stability

____ career and professional

____ social support

____ closest relationships

____ time and schedule

____ learning and personal growth

____ recreation and fun

Life Success Scale Total Score = _____

10–25 = crisis living level

25–50 = unhealthy living level

50–75 = healthy living level

75–100 = optimal living level

How did you score? Were you in an overall crisis or in a healthy place? Did you discover that you are already living out success in some areas? Many of the clients I have coached are pleasantly surprised when they take this profile, because it helps them to immediately gain a larger view of success. Knowing that you are doing well physically or spiritually, have a good sense of ongoing personal growth, have a stable job, or have the admiration and love of others are all indicators of a successful life. Some areas may be weak—don't sweep those under the rug! Begin now to tighten up the areas of weakness to stop losing ground in those areas. The big picture is necessary if you want to gain a sense of what true success means. And remember, if you can't see it and feel it, you won't be able to live it. Author Frank Crane said, "What you want to be eventually, you must be every day. With practice, the quality of your deeds gets down to your soul."

Can you picture it?

Try this exercise to stretch your senses about what success really means to you. Take a breath and then dive into a new way of experiencing success.

Experiencing Success through the Senses

Next in our adventure to achieve lasting success, we will go through a step-by-step plan to outline the things that are most important to you. We will map out the top ten areas of personal success with laser-like accuracy, and you will begin to see where you are naturally strong and where you may be weak. The good, bad, beautiful, and ugly—you have to see it all if you want a complete life of success. The picture of a successful life is amazing, and everyone who comes by will stop to admire how well the colors and designs come together.

Emotions

Can you feel it? Can you already sense a place that you have never been to but know in your heart really exists? Can you sense a feeling of peace and security that you have longed to feel? Can you feel the old hurts and resentments fading away, slipping into a place that doesn't matter anymore? Can you close your eyes and know that your life is good and blessed by God? Can you feel your incredible value and worth? Can you already feel success?

Sight

Can you see it? Can you envision yourself on the porch of a house that you would feel comfortable calling "home"?

Can you see yourself in a healthy body—a strong, fit, rested body? Can you see the smile on the faces of those you love as you hold them close? Can you see yourself crossing off another goal as you continue winning in life? Can you already see success?

Touch

Can you touch it? Can you reach out and grasp the hand of someone reaching back to you? Can you feel the wet, dense soil between your fingers as you plant a rosebush that will produce flowers for many years? Can you feel the smoothness of the gold in the ring that you have wanted to give to the love of your life? Can you feel the softness of the down comforter as you stretch out for another ten minutes of rest? Can you touch success?

Taste

Can you taste it? Can you taste your own hot, salty sweat as you finish up a great workout? Can you taste the warmth of hot chocolate with marshmallows by the fire on a cold night? Can you savor the creamy texture of a rich dessert that was so big you had to split it with a friend? Can you taste the piece of fine chocolate left on your pillow at your favorite resort as you slowly let it melt in your mouth? Can you taste success?

Hearing

Can you hear it? Can you hear the laughter of a child? How about the love and respect of your parents as they tell you how proud they are just to be called your mom and dad? Can you hear the sound of the wind as it fills the sails of the boat you have always wanted to pilot? Can you hear the words whispered into your ears that you have been longing to hear from your marriage partner? Can you hear the praise and applause of your peers as you win yet another award for excellence in your career? Can you already hear the sounds of success?

You Always Have Options

Now that you are beginning to see success in a broader way, you are ready to map out the specific strategy of how to live it out day by day. A fun way to accomplish this is to think through each area with a new vision of what true and lasting success would mean to you. Come back to this exercise again and again, because you will likely see and experience things along the way that help you to "fine tune" your view of success. *Write down your ideas.* You need a written view of success if you are to effectively accomplish it. John Hull, president of the non-profit leadership development company Equip, said it well: "Time is short, so strategy is key." Writing down your personal view of a better life may create difficulty for you. Good! I hope you will be honest enough to list things that will cause you to sweat a bit.

For instance, if your marriage is a 3 but a 9 is where you would like to be, you need to look honestly at your marriage and discover why that score is low. Then consider what you can and cannot immediately do about it and begin to list out your options. One of my all-time favorite coaching phrases is "You always have options." And you really do. So if you take time to do this exercise, you will have begun to develop a personalized action plan to get results in every area of life. It is also important to review your personal view of success regularly and to monitor your results over the course of time. Seeing your success mapped out then actually acted out will give you hope that a better life is possible and in fact is happening day by day.

Your Success Map

Charting your personal strategy for living life well is vital. Remember the rankings from the "Life Success Scale" as you do this extremely important exercise. If you can't envision exactly what success "looks" like to you in a certain area, use your closest estimate so that you at least will have some benchmarks to a better way of living. Put in as much detail as possible. If you get stuck on an area or realize you have never thought about it before, consider the lives of others or ask a close friend for his or her insight. Give this exercise serious consideration, for it will become the map to your new destination of success.

Describe what success means to you by writing in the spaces below:

Physical Health

_____

_____

_____

_____

Emotional Health

_____

_____

_____

_____

Spiritual Health

_____

_____

_____

_____

Financial Stability

_____

_____

_____

_____

Career and Professional

_____

_____

_____

_____

_____

Social Support

_____

_____

_____

_____

Closest Relationships

_____

_____

_____

_____

_____

Time and Schedule

_____

_____

_____

_____

Learning and Personal Growth

_____

_____

_____

_____

_____

Recreation and Fun

_____

_____

_____

_____

Now that you have envisioned what success means to you and have mapped out a strategy for reaching your destination, it is time to unveil the next secret of success, which you will have to master and start implementing immediately. The second secret will help you with the day-to-day routines and behaviors necessary to keep the Success Focus working for you. As business expert Tom Hopkins advises, "There are not many things you need to acquire to get the life you deserve. In fact, each of you . . . possesses all the ingredients necessary for success. But, more than any one thing, you must have a plan."

Running toward Success

Are you ready to live out your dreams? I hope so. Remember that at this point it is common to feel a little nervous. This whirlwind of mental activity is a lot to process at one time. You may have some giant mental blocks in your way. If so, write them down. Don't run away from your fears; instead, begin to run toward them!

The biblical story of David killing the giant Goliath is a perfect example of this. David was just a teenager when he heard Goliath mocking God and the army of Israel. It was more than he could stand! The Israelite soldiers all were scared of this nine-foot "champion" from the enemy army. There was no more fearsome opponent than Goliath. Furthermore, he loudly and arrogantly defied David's God. Goliath's insults stirred up a focused strength inside David that took him to a new level of belief. He knew in his heart that this enemy must die. It was time for David to act. He collected five smooth stones from a nearby brook, then knocked out Goliath by hitting him in the center of his forehead with the first shot from his sling. David cut off the head of his fallen adversary, and the battle was won.

Note this important detail: David started the battle by aggressively running toward his enemy. He charged the giant who had terrified the Israelite army for more than a month. Likely the impact of running, as well as years of practice with a sling, helped David have more velocity to "nail" his target. David instantly became a hero that day, and for the rest of his life people would remember that he had killed mighty Goliath. It was in running toward the fearsome giant that David had the power to destroy him. Likewise, you need to run toward your fears and kill the giant problems that have held you back.

The next part of your journey will be challenging as you confront the giants that have held you back. You will have to run as fast as you can toward things with which you may have been afraid to deal. Know that as you run you are going to break through to a new level of success.

Are you ready for a new script that has you winning this time?

Then run toward secret number two.

THREE

Secret #2

FINDING SUCCESS EVERY DAY

> Success is to be measured not so much by the position that one has reached as by the obstacles which have been overcome while trying to succeed.
>
> —Booker T. Washington

Ted" was one of the most violent men I had ever met, and he had a criminal history to prove it. Nevertheless, he had some amazing insights. For a man who had lost most of what society would call success, his observations were profound. Ted had come to our office for court-ordered counseling about his rage and impulsive outbursts. I was scheduled to meet with him at least once a week for several months to get at the root of why he did such self-destructive things. Why did he keep making the same impulsive mistakes? Why did he continue to do dangerous things? He didn't seem to have a clue, yet I knew that if he stayed sober and we worked together, we could figure it out.

In a Crazy World, the Sane Person Is the Idiot

Ted and I discovered many things in those months of therapy. Evil things had happened to him, and he passed on that evil to others. I began to look for something positive in the middle of his chaotic and bizarre life. One of the gifts he possessed was the ability to confront an issue honestly. Think of it: Here was a man who couldn't keep a job, marriage, or family together. He couldn't and wouldn't pay his financial obligations unless he was chased down, and then he would just creatively dodge his financial responsibilities again the next month. He wouldn't stay away from the unhealthy substances that had contributed to wrecking his life. He continued to pursue women that would end up using him in one way or another. He refused to pay child support to feed his own children or to offer any kindness or financial assistance to his ex-wives. The greatest irony is that if he had spent as much time and energy in any form of gainful employment as he spent in breaking the rules, he could have accomplished much. Instead, he used his energy to avoid any personal responsibility, and he always failed. Although Ted was a failure in nearly every sense of the word, he had great insights into our society and could express them in wonderful stories. He told me one story I have never forgotten. Let me retell it for you here:

There once was a king of a small country who seemed to have it all. He was greatly loved by his family and all the citizens in his kingdom. He was wealthy, powerful, and wise. Everyone respected and admired this king. Because of the partnership he had built with his countrymen, there was a great deal of peace and prosperity in the land. It was as if things couldn't get better.

That is, things seemed perfect until one night when an enemy of the king poisoned the village water supply. Now this poison didn't kill a person instantly; rather, it slowly made one go insane. Over a period of days, the poison could cause a person to become either violent or totally apathetic—and sometimes both. It caused a person not to remember much from his or her past.

The saddest part of this was that the king was the only one who didn't drink from the village well, since he had his own private water supply in his castle. So this king, drinking the pure, unpoisoned water, had no idea why things so radically changed between him and the villagers. Within days they weren't the same. They either sat all day and did nothing or went from place to place creating angry conflicts with everyone they met.

No one figured out that the water was poisoned until one day when the conflict and inactivity levels were almost intolerable. That day the king received a letter from his enemy mocking him. Then he instantly knew what had happened. He finally had all the puzzle pieces of the impossible situation, so he thought that he would just share this news with the villagers to get things back to normal. Perhaps they could work together to figure out a way to solve this crisis in the kingdom. He hurried to tell them about his conclusions, and then he read aloud the note from his enemies. But they didn't seem to care at all.

Not one villager believed him or even wanted to listen. They were actually having fun being irresponsible. They liked their lives of apathy and anger. They didn't want anyone to change things back to a way of life they couldn't remember or even imagine anymore, so nothing changed—nothing except the villagers' total disregard for their king. They didn't trust his authority or like his rules, and they didn't like the consequences he implied would happen if they didn't change. They were so distant and aggressive that the king feared for his very life.

The pressure grew, and it became apparent that the king was going to have to make a decision: leave the kingdom or drink the water.

Think about it. If you were facing the same situation, what would you do? Take a risk to leave everything you knew and move on as a vagabond to start over in some other place? Or take an even bigger risk and drink the poison to be just like everyone else and be named the king of fools?

Poisoned Water, Poisoned People

As Ted finished his story, I sat speechless. Even though he was as far from anyone's view of success as one could be, he had captured the essence of what I believe our society has become. We live in a world that often is hostile to positive influences. Face it: You and I live in a world with poison in the water. It poisons our thinking and behavior, and if we keep drinking it, we will go crazy. Remember, in a crazy world, the sane person is the idiot. The word *crazy* means a deviation from the concept we call "normal." For instance, if you have ever tried to eat responsibly or take nutritional supplements, you may have had someone call you a "health-food nut." The person didn't mean that you were crazy for taking care of your body; rather, it identified you as someone who was quite different, or to say it another way, "abnormal." Consider this for a moment. What if the standard society placed on "normal" thinking was wrong? What if "normal" behavior wasn't healthy at all? What if it was poison? What if everyone was doing something "normal" but it was crazy—would you go along with the crowd?

Society isn't looking out for your good. While I am not a pessimistic, "glass is half empty" thinker, I am not a blindly optimistic, "glass is half full" thinker either. I am a realist—the glass has water in it. Here's the difference. A pessimist thinks that he will one day get mugged. An optimist thinks that he won't get mugged, and a realist is an optimist who got mugged! Bad things happen to good people who are in the wrong place at the wrong time. Simply put, realists notice that success doesn't make the news as much as failure. If you don't believe it, see what sells newspapers. I subscribe to the *Orlando Sentinel*, which has only run out of papers twice in the last five years— once when the top story was about tornadoes that killed forty-two people and later when the paper covered the tragic death of NASCAR driver Dale Earnhardt at the Daytona International Speedway. Consider these success stories that didn't make headlines on the very same days those newspapers sold out.

Dozens of healthy babies were born to create a lot of new grandparents.

Some people walked away from alcoholism and drug addiction.

A young man asked his girlfriend to marry him.

A single mom taught her son that real success isn't marked by buying a hundred-dollar pair of athletic shoes.

Some students listened to their teacher and finally "got it."

A woman was approved for a small business loan.

A lonely man prayed to God about his doubts and fears instead of being "tough" and stuffing it all inside.

A couple decided to work on their distant marriage to find love again.

A middle-aged man faced his fears about trying for a promotion.

A busy executive took off from work to take his daughter to a dance recital.

Thousands of people went to work, motivated to add value to others through their service. In spite of every circumstance, they worked.

Every one of these situations reflects a view of success that will not make the cover of a magazine but is part of a successful life. If you look for success, you will find it all around you in spite of any difficulty.

Melanie Hoover, a businesswoman in Jacksonville, Florida, sent me the following story about the wonder hidden among the obvious. It captures a new view of success.

A group of students were asked to list what they thought were the present Seven Wonders of the World. Though there was some disagreement, the following received the most votes: (1) great pyramids of Egypt, (2) Taj Mahal, (3) Grand Canyon, (4) Panama Canal, (5) Empire State Building, (6) St. Peter's Basilica, (7) Great Wall of China.

While counting up the votes, the teacher noted that one quiet student hadn't turned in his paper yet, so she asked the child if he was having trouble with his list. The reply came, "Yes, a little. I can't quite make up my mind because there are so many." The teacher said, "Well, tell us what you have and maybe we can help." He hesitated, then read, "I think the Seven Wonders of the World are to touch, taste, see, and hear." He hesitated a little, then added, "And to feel, laugh, and love."

The room was silent. Those things we overlook as ordinary are truly wondrous—a gentle reminder that the most precious things in life cannot be bought, but they can be experienced.[1]

Wonder can be experienced every day through tiny events that don't cost a lot. We just have to be alert to see beyond the surface of certain events to discover the deeper meaning. Many people miss out on experiencing success because they aren't looking for anything but cash flow. There is more to life!

Another View of Success

Sadly, this "poisoned water" world brings us many senseless, violent acts. Even as I was sitting here writing, the news reported that a man was murdered this afternoon in the parking lot in front of his business. The killers got away with his money, and life marches on; but his world stopped instantly.

I wish the news media would report the story that happens a few days after a crisis—family members and friends picking up the pieces after the funeral, law enforcement eventually catching up with the bad guys to bring them to justice, the man's children remembering their daddy, other men stepping up to help those children have a positive male role model, church members helping out with carpooling, babysitting, and anything else necessary to help a wounded family.

Coming to terms with the harshness of life and moving forward with the business of living is success. As legendary football coach Lou Holtz said, "Show me someone who has done something worthwhile, and I'll show you someone who has overcome adversity." Success is the courage to face life when it's hard, the courage to move on and not repeat the same old behaviors but to grow into a stronger person, the courage to live a better life in spite of difficulties. How can you move toward the life you were designed to live? Start by asking yourself, "Is my life better today than it was yesterday?"

Events Reveal Emotions

I once saw a T-shirt that said on the front, "I love you more today than yesterday," and on the back it said, "Yesterday you really ticked me off!" If you are "in love" only as long as things are going your way, then you are going to be out of love pretty quickly! Too many people have built their concept of success around this type of thinking. When things go their way, their life is successful, but let life take a twist or turn, and their life is ruined. I have actually had crisis counseling calls from people having panic attacks over a bad haircut. They wanted to sue the beauty shop for punitive damages associated with "ruining my life." Their life was over because of not looking a certain way. Sometimes it is hard for me to deal kindly with self-absorbed shallowness. Part of me wants to say: "Bad haircut! Hey, tell that to a balding guy like me! Some people's hair turns gray and other people's hair just turns loose! Some people have bad hair days and others have no hair days!" Or I want to get really direct and say: "If losing your hair ended your life, then some remarkable people would become suicidal during their chemotherapy. People usually find remarkable bravery when they have to deal with the challenge of cancer. When it is about living or dying, people have to grow up and deal with the real pressures of life, not just how they look. Besides, who are you to complain about such an insignificant thing? It's just hair. Maybe you are just being petty and self-absorbed."

My solution to this type of situation may surprise you. I try to think through where such a statement comes from and react accordingly. I know that the events of life draw out what is in the heart of a person. Events reveal emotions, not create them. Sometimes people say that something made them "so mad." Nope, the anger was already there. What somebody said or did just exposed it. When you try looking at events this way, you will save a lot of hurt feelings and frustration for yourself and others. Remember that petty people do and say petty things. And hurt people end up hurting people; it is a normal dynamic of relationships. By thinking before reacting, we can respond with gentleness and insight instead of with rage or pettiness.

Putting Away Childish Thinking

The first portion of the great love chapter, 1 Corinthians 13, is often quoted at weddings, but usually the minister leaves off at verse 8, where the description of love ends. Verse 11, however, holds another key to having more success in relationships: "When I was a child, I talked like a child, I thought like a child, I reasoned like a child. When I became a man, I put childish ways behind me."

It is childish to think that your life is over when things don't work out. Little girls and boys think they are the center of the universe—the world revolves around them—and that life should always go their way. But life does not always go our way, so we need to get used to it. Learning to manage disappointment is part of growing up, but don't ever get used to living with the feelings of giving up because of setbacks! Never quit!

The purpose of this section is to help you learn to avoid the poison of being an angry or petty self-serving individual and to move on to become a healthy success seeker. Keep reading. Stay with it. You can have a better life, and it can begin right now! I hope that your answer to the question about having more success today than yesterday is similar to that of the great artist Michelangelo when he prayed, "Lord, grant that I may always desire more than I can accomplish."

Destiny or Density?

You were created to accomplish great things—it is your destiny. I cannot hear the word *destiny* without smiling and thinking of the character George McFly from the movie

Back to the Future. You may remember that Michael J. Fox's character, Marty McFly, was transported back to "good old 1955" and through a series of events had to help his parents find each other and fall in love—to help them fulfill their destiny. Cut to the scene in the malt shop. George McFly approaches his love interest with this classic pick-up line: "Lorraine, I'm your *density*." Marty upsets the time-space continuum and totally changes the destiny for his entire family. If you saw the film, you know that it eventually all works out for the McFly clan, although it takes three movies to get there.

Can you imagine though, what would really happen if a guy came up to a gal and said that he was her "density"? Would that really make her go along with him? Or if a gal came up to a guy at the prom and said, "Honey, I'm your worst nightmare and am here to make your next forty years miserable," would he go along? I hope not! That's like the story of the old man who was asked how he and his wife had managed to have a successful marriage without conflict or problems for so many years. He replied, "I took Marge to Phoenix in 1950, and one day I'm going to go back and get her!" While we chuckle at how silly this seems, it is no laughing matter that in real life, density tends to win over destiny too many times.

"All men are idiots and I married their king." If your life is like this slogan from a bumper sticker I saw on the back of a minivan, then you not only found your density, but you are living it. Tired of it yet? No, not the other person. That's too easy a target. You see, when we are unhappy or unfulfilled, we have a tendency to blame other people for our lot in life. Our culture may have poison in the water, but you and I don't have to drink it. Even if everyone else is miserable, we don't have to go along. We can have success in spite of anyone else and in spite of any circumstance.

If you believe that, are you living it? Are you pushing yourself to improve, or are you blaming your unhappiness on your circumstances? Have you begun to deal with the reality of your life, or are you still hoping for a fairy-tale ending like some far-fetched romantic comedy? Have you picked up the broken pieces of your life to sort through them and see what you have to work with, or are you just sitting on top of a pile of debris in shock? Are you becoming more and more successful no matter what happens, or are you stuck on the road to success? Worse yet, are you even on the road?

As you take a minute to consider your life, check some basic issues.

Do you feel stronger and more confident today than this time last year?

Do you have a sense of peace in your soul?

Are your relationships with friends and family healthy?

Do you enjoy your life or just endure it?

Have you reached a level of financial security?

Is your life in balance spiritually, emotionally, and physically?

Are you growing, improving, and living out your potential?

Would your closest friends be able to articulate your future dreams, or would they not even have a clue as to what you desire because you hide it all inside?

Your answers to these questions are a dead giveaway as to which water you have been drinking. If you are afraid to even think about success, I suspect that you have been "beat up" by life. Things have not worked out the way you thought they would. Your personal life as well as professional life may be a mess. You already may have given up on the chance of a better life. Don't give up! Too often people have a powerful sense of being a "have-not" in a world full of "haves." They think that if they weren't born into a powerful family, or haven't won Olympic gold by age eighteen, or haven't had great breaks in life, that it's over for them. They think the script of their life says they will lose, or at most they will always be in the supporting role and not the lead. They think like Charlie Brown when he said, "When my ship comes in, I'll probably be at the airport."

If you have been reading this and thinking that your best could only be to have some minor gains in a slightly better existence, then you have missed a key point. You can find more success than you imagined. Success is not an "out there somewhere" concept; it's inside you. You can rewrite the script of your life to start right now to have a better time in every area. This is a key element of the next secret of success.

 ## The second success secret is that you can find success anywhere.

Success is mental resolve to keep growing through any circumstance. That is why I know that you already hold the keys to success in your hands. You can break away from "normal," or what is expected. Be abnormal! Live beyond what is average. Raise the bar and leap to a higher level than you would have without this secret. Maximize your potential and get ready for even better things in the future.

Moving the Fruit Far from the Tree

I have asked hundreds of people if they wanted their life to be like their parents' life—if they wanted their marriage, finances, career, health, or personal accomplishments to be on par with their family of origin. The overwhelming answer was "No way!" While most people love their parents and respect the fifth commandment in the Bible, "Honor your father and your mother," the majority I have talked with about their family's success record decided to walk a different path. Some who knew dysfunction growing up would rather run away from it and never look back.

Since much of what you know as "normal" is based on the issues of your past, both positive and negative, you may have missed out on how to find the success that is available to you. Maybe your parents never guided you to have a better life than they had. Perhaps their lifestyle implied, "This is as good as it gets, so stop dreaming." You may fear that you cannot break through the roadblocks that stand in the way of you and your dreams. If you have felt like giving up, listen to the words of John F. Kennedy: "Change is the law of life. And those who look only to the past or present are certain to miss the future."

What about you? How are you doing with uncovering the mental power to see success in spite of circumstances? Can you see your roadblocks? Can you see options for moving past them? Can you see success?

Perhaps your false beliefs about success have blocked you from accomplishing more than you ever imagined. If you have lived your life up to this point with the notion that "success just can't happen for me," then I hope that you are beginning to see that it really can. You can leave the "normal" life of losing for a healthy life overflowing with blessings. When you live at a new level, you will feel alive to incredible opportunities. Look for success. Seek it. Live it. Let success happen to you.

You know what the king did when facing the challenge to drink the poisoned water: He didn't drink it—not a drop. Neither should you.

Are you ready to break through to a new way of thinking? Then put down the poison and leave your past behind. It's time to find success. So let's go!

FOUR

WHAT TO DO
WITH THE ELVIS IN YOU

It's not hard to get to the top of the music industry, but it's hard to stay there.

—Elvis Presley

Elvis Aron Presley was born in Tupelo, Mississippi, in 1935. That much you may have known already. However, there are some facts about Elvis's life that you likely don't know, and when you understand what was going on inside this driven young man, you will understand how he was able to become a multimillionaire by his twenty-fifth birthday, create a brand of music that still ranks him as one of the most successful musical performers of all time, and forever change the music industry.

I am going to teach you what I call "the Elvis Factor," which I believe will help you achieve a new view of your potential for success. You will see how important it is to understand and master your drives to prevent your success from being blocked or possibly even destroyed. "The Elvis in you" is a metaphor for understanding your personal passions as well as discovering your life purpose. You will discover how to come to terms with the greatness or grief that can occur when these powerful forces get out of control and are driving your life. Let's learn some key lessons for success from this amazing man.

Elvis University

Former Beatle John Lennon once said, "Nothing really affected me until Elvis." I'm sure there are countless entertainers who would say the same thing. Elvis was amazing. It is nearly overwhelming to see how influential he was during his twenty or so years as an entertainer. It is worth your time to take the tour of Elvis's private estate, Graceland, the next time you are in Memphis, but don't go as a fan. Rather, go as a student of success. The most remarkable part of the tour for me wasn't his lifestyle, although the many walls of awards, including hundreds of gold and platinum records, as well as the jets, motor coaches, and classic cars are impressive. No, the legacy of this man, which draws millions of people to his estate every year, was the most significant part of my visit. Graceland University is open for class, so get ready to learn about monumental accomplishment and crippling personal fears—fears that can steal the success of powerful people and eventually destroy their lives.

Sadly, many popular people won't allow anyone to get close enough to them to coach and guide them toward lasting success. They get burned a time or two and shut out everyone for fear of being used. They protect themselves from the risk of being hurt, but in so doing, they put up a wall that keeps out those who could have blessed them and helped them to live at a higher level. If you don't have a coach, mentor, pastor, priest, rabbi, or godly parents to give you guidance, you will likely make a lot more mistakes along the journey of life—mistakes that cost time, energy, and focus. William Ruffin, one of my college professors, told me to "learn from the mistakes of others, since you can't possibly live long enough to make them all yourself." Elvis trusted few people and was used by many. Maybe that's why he used drugs—perhaps he was trying to control something in his life, since people tend to hypercontrol things when they feel out of control. Maybe that's why he self-destructed at age forty-two.

Elvis is one of the most imitated figures of the last century, so I suspect that you already have an opinion about the man: You either love him or hate him. Whether or not you like his music or the Elvis movie marathons that show up every now and then on classic movie channels, you have to admit that he is one of a kind. Whatever your opinion, my hope is that you don't miss the lessons we can learn from his life.

Elvis's successful branding and marketing principles are still effective almost fifty years later. I want to share the insight of knowing "what to do with the Elvis in you" so that you don't miss out on a powerful principle of personal success and an equally powerful lesson in managing blind ambition and personal fears. I spoke with Elvis trivia specialists John Schneck and Jim Maloof; Elvis impersonator Tom Vianezy;

and Rick Stanley, Elvis's stepbrother, in my quest to discover more about the success of this incredible man. Rick grew up at Graceland, where he lived with his mother and her husband, Vernon Presley. They shared with me their insights about Elvis, which I believe will help you reach success sooner if you learn them.

To Become Great, Study the Lives of Great Achievers

In high school Elvis worked as a movie usher so he could study the lives of stars like James Dean and Marlon Brando. Elvis was driven to be successful. He wanted to be popular and have financial security, and these goals would influence every decision of his young adult life. This unstoppable drive is what makes for the legends in professional sports like Michael Jordan, in politics like John F. Kennedy, in television like Oprah Winfrey, in technology like Bill Gates, and in movie making like Steven Spielberg. They are focused on success and accept nothing less than the best every time. We buy books about them or watch their life stories on biography specials because we want to learn about their success while avoiding their failures.

Elvis worked as a truck driver after his high school graduation and earned enough money to go to the Sun Records studio to make a vanity recording for his mother's birthday. A secretary noticed his energy and created an opportunity for Elvis to meet the studio's owner. The rest is history. Elvis recorded "That's All Right Mama," "Don't Be Cruel," "Love Me Tender," "Hound Dog," "Blue Suede Shoes," and scores of other songs. He eventually would have nearly eighty consecutive million-sellers for RCA records, where at one time his record sales accounted for almost 50 percent of the gross revenues for the entire company. His gospel recordings were re-released from RCA a few years ago and once again had chart-topping sales. His popularity led to his being paid a million dollars per movie (about ten times higher wages than other movie stars of his day) to appear in B-films like *Jailhouse Rock* and *Love Me Tender*. He changed the music industry and became a living legend before he was thirty years old.

But fame can have a hard side, which may have led to the self-destructive excesses that would claim Elvis's life by the age of forty-two. Reflecting on his fame, Elvis said, "I was very lucky. The people were looking for something different, and I came along just in time." I think he was right about the timing, but his success wasn't about luck; it was about hard work. In the early years of his career, he was a very disciplined entertainer and performer. For years he had studied how he wanted to be perceived, and he achieved that image by his early twenties. Author Stephen Leacock once said, "The harder I work, the luckier I get." Elvis was likely the hardest-working performer in the music business when he first started, and his hard work paid huge dividends, because focused work always leads to success.

Research, Then Reinvent, Your Brand

Elvis constantly studied his industry to figure out what would work best in his region and how to successfully brand himself. "The king of rock and roll" continues to be an unmistakable label for Elvis Presley. Someone once said, "The final test of fame is to have a crazy person imagine he is you." If that is the case, then Elvis was the most famous man of his time. Many successful music performers have followed a similar path by branding their music style, dress, and attitude. They include, for instance, Madonna, Michael Jackson, the Beach Boys, Britney Spears, Willie Nelson, *NSYNC, and a host of others who have mastered a particular style and then set out to take it to their respective audiences. Elvis reached the top and set new benchmarks for entertainers to strive toward for generations.

Elvis's success in career, finances, popularity, and business were off the chart. His personal passions drove him to the top of the mountain, but then his lack of restraint and personal boundaries drove him off the cliff at the top of that mountain. What previously had looked like unstoppable success began to unravel and fall apart. Had he kept better focused on business and marketing along with his drive to succeed, he might not have lost the edge in his career and gone into such a terrible slump. If he could have dealt with his inner demons, which led to his overindulgence in drugs, sex, and junk food, he would have been working in Hawaii or Las Vegas long before the need for a "comeback" concert.

I have coached leaders who have an innate ability to read their business environment and react with the elements necessary to capture a significant share of business for their industry. Leaders who can see and understand the climate of their business can always create income opportunities. Seeing success is a gift to those who know how to manage it. Elvis had great instincts on this, and his agent, Colonel Parker, was even better about it. But there is more to success than reaching the top. You have to know how to stay on top or hire someone to coach you to the next level of success. Elvis didn't do that, which may have led to his meteoric self-destructive crash.

Understanding the Elvis Factor

The Elvis Factor is about learning to harness your drives, passions, and ambition. It is having restraint on the dark side of personal ambition that may come with popularity and fame. It is the fire in your soul that burns with a cherry-red glow until it becomes a pure white flame of desire to achieve worthy goals. Historian Charles Sumner said it well: "No true and permanent fame can be found except in labors which promote the happiness of mankind." Mother Teresa had that healthy ambition. So did Abraham Lincoln, Gandhi, and Martin Luther King Jr. You may have had a parent or grandparent who was a servant leader. People with this kind of purpose always change their corner of the world. They are the respected doctors, teachers, firefighters, pastors, nurses, counselors, police officers, coaches, civil servants, and other professionals who add value to others. They don't feel successful if those they serve aren't successful. Many popular entertainers seem to have missed that. Serving people matters most. Helping others will keep you focused, while serving only yourself will likely lead to an empty life of self-indulgence, a trail of broken relationships, failed projects, and superficial accomplishments.

The gold records in the halls of Graceland are impressive, but how much better it might have been if Elvis had slowed down and lived a long life of adding value to others. He missed time with his daughter after being divorced from Priscilla, and he never married again, so he missed the chance for a successful relationship. He seemed more like a prisoner behind the walls of Graceland than a king. He never got to use his musical talent to raise awareness of the needs of the millions of American children struggling in poverty. Providing food, clothing, education, and medical care for children in poverty could have been the legacy of Elvis Presley. He could have been a man with a mission to improve the quality of life for children who grew up in poverty like he did. He could have helped those children to miss despair, prison, drugs, or worse and given them the hope of a brighter future.

Finding Meaning beyond Fame

Look at other stars who lived long enough to have a lasting impact on the lives of those in need. Danny Thomas helped children through St. Jude's Children's Hospital, a tradition that was carried on by his daughter Marlo. Many entertainers have found great meaning in helping with charities that serve people in crisis. Charity groups like Children's Miracle Network, the Make-a-Wish Foundation, Dream Flight, and Give Kids the World, and research organizations for spina bifida, muscular dystrophy, and Parkinson's disease have involved performers like Art Linkletter, Marie Osmond, John Tesh, Burt Reynolds, Jerry Lewis, and Michael J. Fox. The entertainers help people in crisis, but in another powerful way, the entertainers themselves are helped by finding a purpose. Helen Keller understood this concept and said, "Many persons have the wrong idea about what constitutes true happiness. It is not attained through self-gratification but through fidelity to a worthy purpose."

Facing Death Brings Meaning to Life

Facing your own mortality is another way to keep this view of success in balance. A quirky event of an earlier century led to one man coming to terms with managing his life to add value to others. Alfred Nobel was a Swedish chemist who became quite wealthy because of an invention—dynamite. He invented explosive chemicals that were used primarily for weapons of war. As a wealthy and influential man, his life was forever impacted when his brother died and the newspaper mistakenly printed Alfred's obituary instead of his brother's. The newspaper reported that Alfred Nobel was a man who became rich from enabling people to kill one another with destructive weapons.

This view of his life so conflicted with his belief system that he decided to use his fortune to bless humankind instead of only himself. He would seek out and reward notable accomplishments that benefited humanity. The Nobel Prizes have been given out annually for more than a hundred years because of a mistake in a newspaper that led to a man facing what mattered most in his life. He could have become resentful or depressed by the fact that he read his name in the obituaries. But instead of running away or burying his head in the sand, he successfully faced his reality and designed a peace prize that has benefited everyone on the planet. His legacy would forever be attached to building humanity, not destroying it. A success seeker makes the choice of adding value to others in spite of any circumstance.

What would have happened if Elvis had seen his obituary in 1977 before he died? Would he have changed his lifestyle and learned to be a servant leader? What would happen if you read your own obituary? Would you be different? I wish it didn't take cancer, heart disease, the untimely death of a child, divorce, bankruptcy, or the loss of a dear friend for us to figure out that our selfish decisions hurt others and block us from achieving lasting success. Yet if hardship comes and we survive and gain insight for changing our priorities to bring life into balance, then the hardship ends up being a gift that brings greater success.

A Different Kind of King

The perfect example of a successful leader is Jesus Christ. Jesus as a man was remarkable because he was God in flesh dwelling among humans. His life is the personification of holiness and right living. No one has ever had a greater impact on humanity. Jesus had talent, popularity, and the power to do miracles. He balanced his gifts against his life purpose, which kept him focused on one goal—his mission. Listen to his words about true success: "Whoever wants to become great among you must be your servant, and whoever wants to be first must be slave of all. For even the Son of Man did not come to be served, but to serve, and to give his life as a ransom for many" (Mark 10:43–45). Jesus later showed his love for others by laying down his life for them.

Instead of living for our own personal gratification, we should model the kind of life that cares for others and builds success around relationships. This level of character is well beyond fame. It's about being a servant leader rather than a self-serving leader. Jesus walked slowly among the crowd and never avoided being with those he loved; he was always accessible. Study the life of Jesus and you are studying the life of true success, because he kept passion and purpose in perfect balance. When you have the focused energy of personal passion and targeted ambition toward a single goal, you will be unstoppable. Humanitarians living out this kind of success are so totally consumed with accomplishing things for the good of others that their mission is their reason for being.

If you are feeling some pity or loneliness, pull out your Bible and look at how Jesus and his disciples gave everything, including their lives, to impact the world with God's message of hope. It will inspire you and likely ignite your desire to help and not hurt, to love and not leave, to cherish and not criticize, to build dreams instead of destroying them. Read the Book of John and look at how Jesus' every thought, word, and act was about serving others. What a mission! It changed the world and still does to this day. I can't read through the Book of John without being overwhelmed by the power of a focused life for good. It always convicts me to pay attention so that my thoughts, words, and actions stay in line with the purposes I believe I am responsible to manage. Reading the Bible helps me stay focused, but when I ignore it, I drift off into personal agendas that have little thought for others. I have lost too much time working on things that didn't last (or even make any

---

To balance passion with purpose, ask yourself:

- What is going well in your life this week? How are you handling that blessing?
- What problem has consumed your thoughts this week? How are you managing that pressure?
- What have you done this week to serve others?
- What have you done this week to rest?
- Are your passions out of balance, leading you to self-destructive behaviors?
- Are you living a trustworthy life of integrity?

---

sense when I actually slowed down to think about it); I have wasted too much time on projects that were ultimately meaningless. I challenge you to examine your life against your own potential and to answer this question: What was I born to do?

Balancing Passion with Purpose

The Elvis Factor taught me to pay attention to higher purposes than becoming popular or wealthy, to daily live out my values as a healthy and balanced individual with the people I care about, and to have a strong finish in life as my goal. Knowing how dangerous ambition without clear direction can be, I have several friends who use accountability questions to help me stay on course. If you don't have healthy people in your life to ask you these same questions, I challenge you to recruit some! Healthy friends will help you to keep your passions in line with your purpose, resulting in greater success.

I regret the times when insignificant details of my personal agenda get in the way of serving others. They get hurt, and I end up feeling terrible. The worst times are when my kids get hurt. How could I so selfishly neglect their needs to accomplish some meaningless task? Yet I have done it, and likely so have you. Holding my children and seeking their forgiveness for hurting their feelings is hard. But it is the path to healing for them and for me too. I have learned to face and deal with issues directly, to learn from mistakes and hopefully not repeat them. One of the hardest lessons for me is remembering that to choose something good may cost the best. That is, some activities are worthy and good but not best, and success seekers are always looking for the best. Always.

Self-Improve or Self-Destruct

Elvis's behavior gradually became self-destructive like a slow "suicide." Hopefully you are well beyond the dangerous issues that led to the early deaths of celebrities like Elvis, John Belushi, and Marilyn Monroe. Even if you aren't involved in a "party till you drop" lifestyle of drugs, sex, and alcohol, your success may be hindered by little roadblocks like sleep loss, poor health from a lack of exercise, or a lack of personal accountability for living a life of purpose. Big or little roadblocks can steal your success, so deal with them as aggressively as if you are fighting for your life! You either self-improve or end up self-destructing, so actively begin to face those roadblocks.

Theologian Oswald Chambers taught, "Every man is made to reach out beyond his grasp." One of the main elements of the Elvis Factor is to be boldly ambitious and aggressively chase down your dreams. Keeping your ambition balanced with meaning and the things that matter most is key. You have drives and passions—everyone does. You were born with a purpose given by a God who loves you and specially designed you. When this purpose is discovered and then ignited by passion, it will carry you like a rocket to places that will amaze you. With clear guidance, strong restraints, and structured boundaries, this is one of the most exciting aspects of life. But without guidance or restraint, it will kill you and likely others too.

Author Steve Brown tells a whimsical story that always makes me smile. "When it comes my time to die, I want to go quietly in my sleep, like my grandfather. Not screaming, yelling, and crying like the other people in the car." If you don't take the time to study, uncover, manage, and then master your passions and drives, you will end up driving over the cliff and hurting yourself and anyone with you. Elvis drove off the cliff. If you don't learn from his mistakes, you might drive over the edge as well. I saw a television commercial showing a guy driving a car off a cliff and crashing onto the ground below. Several people watch him crash and say, "What was he thinking?" as they climb into their "safe" car. Many people drive over the edge of their lives because they just don't think. While the commercial is to draw attention to driving safer cars, we can use it as a reminder to study and learn from the strengths and weaknesses of others. If you spend time thinking about your life purpose and balance that with your life passions, you will be on a new path, one that takes you to a destination of success.

The Celebrity Self-destruction Cycle

Elvis Presley, a young man from rural Mississippi, had a dream and ended up changing the face of the music industry forever. He started singing in church and went on to become the king of rock and roll. He went on to make dozens of movies and television specials and shattered every standard for profitability in record sales. When he got beyond a certain point, his ambition led to his destruction. As his fame grew, it seemed that his inner desperation did as well. His mother's death, a failed marriage, loss of custody of his daughter, and drug addiction led to an intense loss of purpose and direction. Elvis's passions to achieve died, and he began to self-destruct and crash with the same velocity with which he had skyrocketed to the top. Alexander Pope said, "Fame can never make us lie down contentedly on a deathbed." Drugs often go with despair as an attempt to cover up the pain or emptiness inside that fame can never fill. Learn the lesson that success is more than popularity or wealth. When you consider the lives of many celebrities, you see the same cycle:

Dreams → Hard Work → Popularity →
Fame → Self-destruction

The Elvis Factor is to see the amazing level of greatness and potential inside of you. It is about dreams with bold ambition and powerful energy focused on winning the prize. It is living aggressively while being wary of the dangers of self-destruction that always lurk in the shadows. If you don't master all seven secrets of success, you face the danger that your accomplishments will lead you to arrogance and self-destruction. There are bookshelves full of stories about broken lives that ended that way. Pick up a two-year-old copy of *People* magazine and see who was popular back then but then lost popularity because of self-destruction. It could happen to you if you ignore this lesson. Accomplishing greatness without balancing the other elements of a successful life can lead to destruction. However, if you learn to keep the success secrets in balance, each "win" helps fuel the elements necessary to truly enjoy life. To win with a balanced and complete life is to be one of the richest of the rich and wisest of the wise, because you are rich in relationships and wise in what matters most.

Avoiding the Dark Side of Success

Unbridled success can have a dark side that leads to destruction. Lasting success includes others and has room for every event, circumstance, and obstacle. Life is hard, but God is good. This is a spiritual lesson about true success that will protect you from the deep emptiness that comes when you have great accomplishments in a few areas and failures in others. Empty people end up going to drugs, alcohol, gambling, sex, or food to avoid the pain of their empty lives. Sometimes they chase money, popularity, materialism, or get-rich-quick schemes for relief.

Think about this phrase again: "Life is hard, but God is good." God has a purpose in the hardship of your life, either from your childhood pain or current problems. These difficulties create pressure, which shapes you into a person of character and compassion even now. Elvis died young and missed out on lasting success. Missing the lessons from his life could cost you the same: everything. Learning them could give you the same: everything.

Are you ready to learn the next lesson of a successful life?

Then let's "rock on" together as we discover the next secret!

PART 2

THE SUCCESS FEAR

Twenty years from now you will be more disappointed by the things you didn't do than by the ones you did. So throw off the bowlines. Sail away from the safe harbor. Catch the trade winds in your sails. Explore. Dream. Discover!

—Mark Twain

FIVE

FACING YOUR SUCCESS FEARS

To conquer fear is the beginning of wisdom.

—Bertrand Russell

"You can't do it, and you never will." How many potential leaders have been crushed by those eight words? Hundreds? No, probably more like hundreds of millions. The worst part is that it could happen to you if you aren't careful. Maybe you think that it already has—but if so, think again. You control your choices, which means that you control your destiny more than you may have thought. It is possible to break the pattern of how you have been living and move into a better way of life. You just have to get past one thing: the "dark side" of your soul. It has been hurting you for years by silently stealing away your motivation and creative energy, and you never even knew it.

In this part of our journey toward success, you will face your deepest fears. You may be thinking that this is a good place to put down the book and run! Perhaps—but you must run *toward* fear. You are bigger than your success fears; you just need to run toward those fears to believe it for yourself. When you courageously turn around to face and deal with your life, you will break through to a new level of thinking. Every time you stare down your fears, a powerful thing will begin to happen: You will gain the unshakable confidence of a success seeker! To begin this revolutionary process, ask yourself:

Am I ready to get honest and move to a better way of life?

Am I ready to stare down the fears that have held me back?

Am I ready to use the "Zilla Factor"?

When you shine the light of truth onto your darkest fears, the darkness disappears, as does the fear. When my kids used to be afraid of bugs and spiders, I showed them how they were much bigger than the bug and therefore didn't need to be afraid. To the critter, they were Godzilla sized, and Godzilla never loses! You can learn to use the "Zilla Factor" as you tackle your troubles. Become Shirley-zilla or Robert-zilla to conquer the fears that lurk in the darkness of your soul! If you could honestly see what is holding you back and how small it is, you would immediately take action. You would feel motivated to focus your energy and begin to make radical changes. Think of how many goals you would accomplish if only you weren't afraid to try.

Two Groups to Choose From

There are two groups to consider. Call them "S-Group" for the successful and "F-Group" for the fearful. If you are like the innovative problem solvers of S-Group, this section will help create the momentum you have been missing to break through to a new level of success. How? How can you consistently get better in spite of any circumstance? You have to learn to turn on the lightbulb of your mind. Remember, the darker the situation, the easier it is to find that light! As you illuminate your success fears, you can really see what's going on and then know how to respond effectively.

Here are the characteristics of S-Group:

- They learn to face things head-on and to search out the missing links to a better way of life.
- They don't run away from painful reality; instead, they try to find insight to illuminate the darkness of their difficult situation.
- They regularly look for any darkness in their souls so they can bring the light of truth to those areas as well.
- They know they don't know everything, so they are frequently asking others for advice, guidance, coaching, and counsel.

S-Group has one more essential quality. They read, study, and list their options on paper. Their lists are lengthy, but their passion to find the light of success in spite of the circumstances drives them on in their search of a better way. They know that good research brings great results. These are the men and women you will read about in *Biography* magazine, because they learned the secrets to press on when everything seemed to be going against them. S-Group is full of innovative leaders, and there is room for you too!

The S-Group's "success in spite of the odds" thinking is based on a combination of insight from others, previous failures or successes, and learning to trust their "gut-level" intuition. The people of S-Group slowly and carefully develop a detailed plan. Daily discipline is their greatest tool to finding and living success, because once they have a plan, they work it every day. They pray a great deal and follow God's guidance in Scripture as well as listen to God's insight through wise counsel. Do they become successful overnight? No. It is a process that takes a while, but as the old saying goes, "Inch by inch, it's a cinch."

Is it worth it? Yes. The S-Group enjoy a better quality of life than most people because they are lifelong learners and find joy in spite of circumstances. If you could sit down with the energized people of S-Group to discuss their life story, it would read like an action-packed adventure novel. This group has such a great time in life because they are living out the seven secrets of *Destination Success*. You will begin to have the pleasurable experience called "living" instead of the pain of barely "existing." When you get past your fears of the future, you will experience a better today because you will find deeper meaning and fulfillment with every activity.

F-Group has a more difficult experience in life. Here are some of their characteristics:

- They dismiss these success strategies, because it feels just like any other day of wandering through the darkness of their long-dead dreams.
- They have been beat down and discouraged for a long time, maybe most of their lives. Nothing ever works out for them.
- It hurts to try again, because everything they feel inside leads them to believe that trying will just lead to more hurt and rejection.

Be careful about criticizing F-Group for giving up on a better life. They have been stepped on by life and have a lot of pain. They have failed one too many times and often are too tired to try again. They have fought against the darkness, and the darkness seems to be winning. F-Group has given up. They have lived in darkness for so long that now they are afraid of the light.

The Power of Light

Kind of says it all, doesn't it? The F-Group are afraid of the light, because light exposes flaws and reveals weaknesses. Light brings out the truth. I have been in dozens of television studios through the years to do interviews and am always amazed at the power of light and darkness. Studios are very dark places. The walls, floor, and ceiling are usually painted the darkest black you can imagine. It literally soaks up any stray light. Tony DiGirolamo is an Emmy award–winning television light designer. He can make you look intense or relaxed just by changing the lighting. He is respected as a leader in his industry because he knows the power of light. He knows how to soften a television set to remove shadows, how to "warm" a set for a personal interview, or how to heighten the awareness and attention of a news viewer by bringing in more focused light.

Light has the power to show you what's really there. Studio lighting can make you look better if a pro like Tony is at the controls, or it can make you look washed out if it is too bright. You know those big mirrors at department store cosmetic counters—the kind with big, bright lights attached to them? There is a profit motive behind those bright magnification mirrors. They reveal your blemishes and flaws so you'll be apt to buy more makeup. You don't look that bad to others, but the mirror doesn't lie, right? Mirrors only show what's there, and if magnified, ten times more of what's there.

Likewise, the light of truth shows what's inside you. Allowing that light to shine into your heart and soul is a necessary part of finding and living success. If you have never allowed the light of truth to shine into the darkest parts of your soul, get ready to experience some tears. Brightness shining into the dark and hidden corners of your mind will bring tears of pain, and viewing how your fears have held you back will bring tears of regret. This poem by an unknown author says it well:

The Dream Stealers

Throughout my life, my friends and folks have offered me advice.
And though they meant the best for me, it often wasn't nice.

They'd always say my plans were just more crazy
  schemes.
And every time I listened, I let them steal my
  dreams.

I guess they feared, in case I failed, that I really
  shouldn't try.
So I never spread my wings and never learned to
  fly.

But they're just folks who only see the world the
  way it seems,
And I'm no longer going to let those people steal
  my dreams.

Are you tired of letting others steal your dreams? Then you
are ready to tackle some difficult issues that you may have
been avoiding for years. I have walked with thousands of
people through the journey of coming to the light by dealing
with painful problems and life pressures. I have heard their
stories. I have felt the desperation of the lonely souls who have
totally abandoned the concept of a better life. I have looked
into the hollow eyes of someone who believed that life was
over because of too many bad choices with sex, drugs, and
alcohol. I have heard about the depression and anxiety that
come from countless problems and dark days. I have wept
with people as they have told me about the terrible things
they have endured. I have winced while listening to stories
of countless tragedies and hardships. Sometimes it has been
hard to walk through the painful issues and hear about the
dreadful things that have happened to them.

Perhaps you can identify with these struggles of coming to the light. Below is a coaching worksheet I use to help people begin the journey from F-Group to S-Group. See if any of these questions describes how you sometimes feel. Remember, the value of living in the light only comes when you are honest, so don't hold back on evaluating your potential success fears.

Are You Blocked from a Successful Life?

Check off any of these statements that apply to your life.

_____ Are you chronically worried about money or debt?

_____ Have you given up on ever having a healthy and fit body?

_____ Are you longing to find a "true love" but constantly being hurt?

_____ Do you sometimes feel intense loneliness or rejection?

_____ Are you afraid that your job will suddenly end?

_____ Have you ever felt that your life was out of control?

_____ Are you panic-stricken when you think about retirement?

_____ Do you get "lost" in novels or movies about people finding happiness?

_____ Are you always stressed out, mad, or depressed about something?

_____ Have you lost your drive to try again to reach your dreams and goals?

_____ Are your best days in life behind you?

_____ Do you ever wonder if God is really there or even cares about you?

_____ Total checked

Green Zone: 1–4 = *Part of your life is blocked by a Success Fear.*
This is a common stage experienced by many people at various times. If you are in this category, then let's partner together to work through a few areas to maximize your success. As you are more and more successful, you can reach out to mentor and empower others with your newfound insights.

Yellow Zone: 4–8 = *You are approaching a crisis level.*
This category shows that about half of the areas of your life are in some type of crisis. You will need a lot of strategic support and realistic coping skills to make it out of this hazardous zone and back into the growth and security available in the green zone. This needs to be a high priority in your daily life and routines.

Red Zone: 8–12 = *You are near a complete breakdown.*
This stage indicates that your life is virtually out of control. You cannot make it out of the dangerous red zone without strategic help and coping skills. You may need professional assistance to get you on the "fast track" of a better life—including financial, emotional, spiritual, and physical guidance. Getting your life back under control demands your complete focus to prevent your life from going into a major meltdown. Take this seriously! Your quality of life and future success depend on taking immediate action to get your life under control.

Before you panic, let me remind you that any of these feelings are "normal" to experience. These major roadblocks are common, which is why we have come to call the principles for moving beyond them "secrets" of success. But notice I said "normal," not "healthy." These are serious indicators of problems, pressures, and obstacles to the healthy life you want to live.

Failures Get Despondent, Success Seekers Get Direction

Don't settle for the idea that "everyone else feels this way, so I'll just sit back with them and be comfortable too." No, that is the way a "loser" would talk. That is the thinking of the fearful who don't want to deal with issues that are blocking their success. If you want to live in the light of the truth, flag this page so that you can refer to it again and again. As you and I journey through this section of overcoming your success fears, let's keep your specific roadblocks in mind. That way we can target the areas that need the most attention to help you achieve the maximum results in moving forward to a healthier way of life.

In my early years as a counselor I learned the value of "weeping with those who weep," because they need to experience comfort before they can hear correction. I used to wonder how these dear people could even get up to try again. The secret is that the majority of people in F-Group really do want to change. They don't want to stay lost in a sad life full of pain and problems.

I have good news for the F-Group. You don't have to stay afraid. You don't have to live in the shadows. You don't have to stay in the "mental manure" that was dumped on you. You can change. You can climb out of the mess of broken pieces and go on to a new place of success. Businessman Donald Trump understood that when he said, "You will never be poor as long as you have hope." Digging in with hope and courage to try again will show that you are serious about success. If life has knocked you down, of course you are afraid—it hurts! Stay put until you get a strategic plan, adequate support, and

---

Seeking Professional Help

If your scores placed you at the complete breakdown level, call one of the professional counseling groups listed below. I partner with these groups and know that they model clinical excellence and spiritual insight. Thousands of qualified professionals in the United States specialize in solution-focused therapy. Many offer coaching services as well.

American Association of Christian Counselors
    (800) 5-COUNSEL or www.aacc.net
Focus on the Family
    (800) A FAMILY or www.family.org
New Life Clinics
    (800) NEW LIFE or www.newlife.com

---

some skills to help you cope. Once you have those things going for you, they will protect you from repeating the same mistakes. Use this strategy effectively so that when you get up, you stay up. This second step toward the life you have been looking for will deal with each of those key elements needed to overcome your success fears.

If you are near breakdown and just too tired to try again, hang in there! Your life has been hard, and you will need a higher level of care and support. Calling a professional to help you get back on track is a good idea. Start by calling your pastor, priest, or rabbi and discussing your difficulties, because spiritual support is the best place to begin to tackle major life problems. And don't miss out on the value of discussing your physical well-being with your family doctor, who can rule out any major health problems. Finally, consider the value of reaching out to a professional therapist.

This concept is called a "treatment team," and it is the best way to break through your problems. Being surrounded by caring people and committed professionals is a safe place to be. No one can make it through this world without the help of others. Don't go it alone! Get a coach, a counselor, a mentor, a trusted friend—buy a German shepherd! Do something to avoid going through life alone. One of the greatest roadblocks to a life of true success is isolation. Mother Teresa was once asked about her view of the biggest problem in the United States. Some guessed that she would say abortion, pornography, debt, adultery, poverty, divorce, or homelessness. But, no, she said, "The single greatest problem facing the people of the United States is loneliness."

Mired in the Mud of Personal Misery

I travel to many regions of our country as a communicator. As part of my preparation to speak, I pay attention to how people look to see if they are enjoying life in their community or corporate culture. I always see empty and lonely looks on the faces of people going about their daily tasks. Their shoulders are stooped, their smiles are gone, and their energy is zapped. I have seen it in airports, restaurants, and shopping centers and on subways and city streets. Everywhere I see the hollow looks of lonely souls that seem to shout out, "I have given up on a better life. Just leave me alone!"

Maybe it's because of what I do, but I notice those who are fearful of trying again, of living a better life, of being successful. It's as if they are mired in the mud of personal misery. It doesn't have to be that way, because deep inside of every person I've counseled I've seen an element of hope—hope that he or she could move from a position of "Can't do it" to "Yes, I can!" It may have been only a spark, but once discovered and ignited, it started a forest fire of desire to live at a higher level.

Remember that every success seeker in S-Group started out in the trampled F-Group. That's the way life works. No one can make success happen for you, and even if someone could, it wouldn't last. Every successful person once had some intense fear of stretching his or her wings and breaking out of the mold. It's normal to wonder, and it's reasonable to question the reasons behind why things don't change. The dedicated inventors and scientists who have improved the world learned to think about change in a new way, and you can too.

Life Instead of Death Was His Goal—Life Won!

The famed medical researcher Louis Pasteur said, "In the field of observation, chance favors the prepared mind." Pasteur continually studied what some believed to be impossible in medicine and found a new way. He turned the "can't cure," dreaded diseases of his century into robust wellness for billions of people worldwide. Pasteur changed the world because he moved past "can't" thinking to living out the vision of successfully bringing health to humankind. He had to face impossible odds of doubt and peer rejection to accomplish his goal. How ironic that the whole world wanted a cure for disease and longed for a solution to infection yet doubted that it would ever happen. He must have heard a thousand times, "Infection leads to disease, and disease leads to death.

Everyone is going to get sick. Everyone is going to die. That's the way it is, Louis. Just give up and get used to it."

Humans can learn to accept pain as a way of life, to just "live with it" and go on without "rocking the boat" of mediocrity. Thank God that Louis Pasteur saw it differently. He saw health instead of death. His life passion was to find a cure, and he will be remembered forever as a successful humanitarian because of his desire to discover a cure and then bring it to others. Penicillin has become the answer to the prayers of millions of parents who have stayed up all night placing cold compresses on a child's forehead. It has given sons and daughters a chance to fight infection instead of succumbing to a high fever that slowly saps the life out of little bodies. Pasteur's seeing life instead of death meant that children would have a future of building tree forts and playing hide-and-go-seek instead of dying young, as did so many children of his era. Thank God, life won! It is likely that you and your family have benefited from a healthier life because of his desire for all humans to have a life of wellness instead of disease.

Maybe you will be like Pasteur and will be the one to find a cure for cancer, AIDS, or diabetes. I know this much: It will take courage to break out of your fears to move toward a better life. That's why so many people in the F-Group exist in the shadow of their doubts. They are stuck on the cul-de-sac of life. It's a comfortable trip, but they are just driving around in circles waiting for the mystical day to come when things will work out for them and they will have a better life. If you are waiting for that one day, you are not alone. Fantasy thinking sells plenty of lottery and movie tickets, but those who engage in it end up barely surviving. You must make an aggressive move to join the S-Group. And I believe that this is your time.

Break Down or Break Through?

I have seen two distinct reactions to the challenge to confront one's fears. One group has a *breakdown* while the other group has a *breakthrough*. The doubts, insecurities, and fears we are about to deal with may rip open the deepest wounds in your life, causing hurt and pain, but this is a necessary part of breaking through to a new level. If you have never faced your fears, then this is very scary stuff, which is why you have been immobilized for so long. Don't run away. This is your place. This is your time. The third secret will help you break the patterns of the past that have been stopping you for far too long. You can have success even if all you have ever known is "can't do it" thinking.

Move Beyond Success Fears with a New Vision

Can you see strength coming back to your dreams?

Can you see the path to the life that you have always wanted?

Can you envision a life of wellness, peace, and prosperity?

If you can't, then read on, because the third secret to success may be the breakthrough that you have been missing.

Now can you rephrase the earlier "can't" statement into this seven-word sentence: "I can do it and always will"? Can you see yourself saying this? More important, can you picture yourself living it? The dreams and visions of success that you and I have been building together will never happen if you don't face your fears. Facing your fears means that you have to consider

the part of you that is on self-destruct

the old tapes

the past failures

the hidden doubts

the deepest insecurities

the demons inside

the *L* on your forehead you have been trying to cover up

Whatever you call it, there is part of you that limits, blocks, or tries to destroy any real and lasting success. It stops your growth cold and eventually kills any future visions of greatness. When creativity and personal belief begin to die, your momentum is headed downhill, and instead of using your energy to build a better way of life, you use it for "sucking air" just to stay alive.

Turning Barriers into Bridges

The mindset of failure has been a barrier on your journey to success, so begin now to have a new attitude of "can do it" as I coach you about breaking through your barriers and building a new bridge to the successful life you have been dreaming about. God wants you to have a life radiant with his blessings, a brighter future than you could ever imagine back in the dark cave of your fears. Come out to enjoy life in the light! Start right now to break through your barriers and cross over the bridge to discover a whole new world of blessings. Consider the quality of life you could enjoy with these characteristics of success.

a healthy body
an intimate marriage
exotic vacations
strong faith in God
loving children
a great job
emotional strength
connection to extended family
advanced educational degrees
financial security
respect of coworkers
a comfortable home
a better way of life

As good as these things sound, many people are afraid of coming out of the darkness into a life of blessing because it means breaking out of the mold. To move beyond the way things are to a new level is hard, because it took you a lifetime to build that mold. Part of you is comfortable in the darkness. Part of you has given up and accepted "that's the way it is," and you have stopped trying to grow to a new level.

It is sort of like rock climbing. I once spent an afternoon watching some young adults "free climb" at a beautiful park called Garden of the Gods in Colorado Springs. They seemed fearless as they scurried up and over a hundred-foot natural rock wall. They were agile and aggressive in their quest to see who could get to the top the fastest. It seemed that they barely had to look for hand- or footholds as they quickly moved up the face of the rock. So I decided to give it a try—no, not on sheer rock cliffs, but on a three-story climbing platform designed for practice climbing. Ouch! Even with the benefit of the man-made grips it was hard. Gravity kept pulling me away from the wall, and there never seemed to be a grip right where I wanted one. My arms turned into Jell-O after just a few attempts. I was feeling like the "sissy man" described by Hans and Franz in the *Saturday Night Live* sketches and wishing I had taken time to listen to those muscular guys with their constant advice of going to the gym to "Pump you up!" Part of me felt crazy for even trying to climb up to the next level—yet part of me felt exhilarated when I got there!

Climbing is hard, but that's the only way you can get to the top. Growing is hard, but that's the only way you get to a better life. You may have been dragging some fears with you for decades, so it will take some time to get them under control and then more time to master them. Moving up a level in any area of life is going to take a focused strategy with concentrated effort, and it's not going to happen quickly. But every day will be more fulfilling as you enjoy life as a success seeker. So now let's get past those fears. Are you ready? Strap on your harness; it's time to climb!

SIX

Secret #3

BUILDING SUCCESS BY MASTERING YOURSELF

The mold of our fortunes is in our own hands.

—Sir Francis Bacon

Filmmaker and actor Woody Allen once said, "Fifty percent of success in life is just showing up." But you'll have to do a whole lot more than just show up to capture and keep the third of the seven secrets of success. Attaining a meaningful life is going to be an uphill climb, but it will be worth every drop of sweat and every bit of effort! Are you ready? Here's the third secret of success:

The third success secret is to get past your self-imposed limits.

When people hit their mental barriers, they're done. Dried up. Dead. Gone. Call the fat lady out to sing, because their life, relationships, career, and world are finished. When you create limits in your mind, you can never get past them. When you believe something to be "impossible," you will leave it alone. You will give up and not even try anymore. No one can talk you into trying again, because you will think, "Why bother; it just can't be done."

You may have had great frustration in the past dealing with friends or business associates over this issue. Perhaps you tried to convince them that they could do something, that they had the potential, only to watch them give up. The same thing happens to you when your self-imposed limits get in the way, because these limits are your biggest roadblocks to a successful life. Facing and moving beyond those limits are going to be the greatest challenges to the life you have wanted. Why? Because you believe those limitations to be real and virtually impossible to change.

People get stuck in an old habit and sometimes just don't know how to get past it. I heard a story about a preacher who was making his rounds on a bicycle when he came upon a little boy trying to sell a lawn mower. "How much do you want for the mower?" asked the preacher. "I just want enough money to go out and buy me a bicycle," said the little boy. After a moment of prayerful consideration, the preacher asked, "Will you take my bike in trade for it?" The little boy asked if he could try it out first, and after riding the bike around a little while said, "Mister, you've got yourself a deal." The preacher took the mower and began to try to crank it. He pulled on the rope a few times with no response. He called the little boy over and said, "I can't get this mower to start." The little boy said, "That's because you have to cuss at it to get it started." The preacher said, "I've been a minister for twenty-five years; I don't even remember how to curse." The little boy looked at him happily and said, "Just keep pulling on that rope. It'll come back to ya." While this story always makes me laugh, it is my hope that you will move beyond your old habits, fears, and doubts without those self-defeating behaviors coming back.

Impossible Becomes Possible

Thousands of things once thought unattainable are now commonplace, because when the first person shattered the "impossible" barrier, anything became possible. Consider how runners viewed the four-minute mile. A hundred years ago it was impossible and everyone knew it. More significantly, every athlete lived by that well-known limitation. The only possible exception was when a mountain man was being chased by a raging grizzly bear; he might have forgotten about the four-minute limitation while trying to save his skin! Doctors of that era even had said that the human body couldn't go faster than four minutes a mile without doing harm to vital organs. The four-minute mark stood strong until Roger Bannister broke through the barrier and then was followed by thousands of others. Now a four-minute mile is no big deal! Once the self-imposed limits were shattered, everyone saw that it could be done and went about finding the success that was waiting on the other side of the limitation that was defined by history.

The same thing happened to Mark McGuire, the baseball power hitter for the St. Louis Cardinals who challenged the decades-old record for the most home runs in a single season. There was incredible excitement as he approached and then shattered a record set thirty years earlier by Roger Maris. McGuire went on to further establish a new record that season. Baseball fans went wild. The impossible in their sport had now become possible. It could be done. Someone had made it to the top of the summit and looked over into baseball's promised land. Now every player could see a new horizon of home run opportunities. Just two years later, slugger Barry Bonds would break McGuire's record with seventy-one home runs. Who knows when the home run record will be shattered again? I can tell you this much though: It will fall. It has to. Records will be broken every time someone gets past his or her self-imposed limitations. Watch for it. Expect it. Enjoy it!

Heroes Create New Visions of Success

Every swing power hitters take will remind them of the possibility of being the next Babe Ruth, Roger Maris, Mark McGuire, or Barry Bonds. Even little kids playing in tee-ball leagues think about greatness. Often they will stand in line for an hour to get an autograph from their favorite baseball hero. At major league ballparks around the country, you can see kids who want to be like their heroes. Even though they may be only six years old, they get the baseball cards, shirts, shoes, hats, and gloves of their favorite players because they too aspire to greatness as a player. These little guys and gals believe they can be as big, fast, strong, and successful as their heroes. Kids need positive role models, because those models shape what they desire to be like in the future.

Granted, those kids may not be playing at Wrigley Field, but it feels like greatness to them just the same. If you don't believe this, then go to a Little League field and watch the kids play. Most aren't very good and are playing to have fun, which is how it should be. Those who have been pushed into it by an overzealous parent are easy to spot, because they aren't having fun at all! However, if you watch carefully, you will always see a few guys or gals just itching to hit or field that ball. They are in constant training to be a powerful player. They want to push the limit and be all they can be as athletes. It's fun to watch that kind of discipline on the field. While these kids may not move on to play for the majors, they are experiencing the success of totally giving themselves to the game.

The Power of "Why?"

Small children don't know that they can't do certain things, which is why they can play with such power and confidence. They don't know that many things in life are labeled "can't," so they try anything, often to their own peril! They don't know that they can't put on their Superman pajamas and jump off the top bunk to fly through the house! They may believe that anything is possible. The thinking of small children is radical and mind-boggling. They ask "Why?" constantly, because they can automatically see outside the box of limitations you and I often place on things without even realizing it. My friend John Maxwell teaches the following principle about creative thinking ability.

Birth to age 7	Children ask, "Why?"
Ages 7 to 17	Young people ask, "Why not?"
Ages 17 to 80	Adults simply say, "Because."

What a world it would be if adults started thinking creatively about why things are the way they are and challenging the self-imposed limits! Do you know what would happen? They would have the amazingly high energy and creative enthusiasm of six-year-olds. Have you ever watched creative people working? They work with the energy of ten people! They are having the time of their lives! If you started thinking beyond your self-imposed fears of a successful life, you would see radical changes in your life as well.

Breaking the Fear Barrier

When people think beyond their fears, records are broken again and again. Becoming focused on giving your best to whatever you are doing will allow you to do amazing things! Consider the impact on our culture if individuals charged through their own fear barriers.

- Business profits would soar, because leaders would raise the bar of their profession to excellence in every product and service offered. Profits always follow satisfied customers.

- Hospital staffs would be committed to the wellness of their patients, and health care would offer quality services to everyone through a continuum of care.
- Family life would improve because dysfunctional outbursts of anger and chronic arguments would disappear as family members lived out the important values of a peaceful home environment.
- Customer satisfaction would be so high that complaint departments would be replaced with departments that track new records in customer service.
- Record-breaking sales would become a regular feature of local newspapers, and the Wall Street analysts on MSNBC would spend their time discussing the vast potential of companies instead of yet another shocking corporate bankruptcy.
- Political leaders would be respected with the trust and integrity earned by public servants, and criminal scandals would be something that only happened in other countries that followed the philosophy of greed instead of greatness.

While these conclusions may seem impossible to some, you are learning that success seekers break barriers of fear, frustration, and failure to find a better quality of life. When you take ownership for your behavior and live responsibly, tremendous change happens. And those changes will bring remarkable results to your personal life, home, and business.

The Message of the Marble

The *Johnson City Press*, a newspaper outside Knoxville, Tennessee, reported a story about breaking the greed barrier in business. The article was titled "Losing Marbles Frowned Upon." The reporter, John Thompson, used the popular phrase "Don't lose your marbles" as a catchy way of sharing an innovative customer service strategy. While "losing your marbles" is a way to express going crazy, "hanging on to your marble" is a completely different concept that has impacted an international corporation. Jesse Shwayder, who believed that the best way to do business was to treat others the way you would like to be treated, founded the Shwayder Trunk Manufacturing Company. You may already know his philosophy as the Golden Rule. Christ proclaimed it to his followers as "Do to others what you would have them do to you" (Matt. 7:12).

Traditionally, every new employee of Mr. Shwayder's company is given a marble with a golden band imprinted with Matthew 7:12. If a person loses his marble, they are expected to purchase a dozen, keep one, and distribute the remaining ones to others while telling the important story of the Golden Rule. Shwayder said:

> We have found, for practical as well as moral reasons, the Golden Rule is the finest program we could adopt. The Golden Rule has more power than the atomic bomb. With its help, men still can work wonders. If the Golden Rule were adopted by the nations of the world, people would live differently. Wars wouldn't happen, because peace on earth would replace the power struggle of ego-driven dictators. Business profits would soar, because customers would

know that someone, somewhere was watching out for their best interests.

Wow! I am glad that I have used luggage from the Shwayder Trunk Manufacturing Company for years. By the way, you probably have too, because this company eventually became known as Samsonite. You can trust a company with a commitment to treating you the way they would want to be treated. Jesse Shwayder was wise to see the power of living a life of serving others and wiser still to pass along that advice to his corporate culture. Living out the Golden Rule is a great way to find success over your self-imposed limitations. You begin to live differently because something great is happening inside of you. You are moving beyond your fears to become a servant leader. The Golden Rule is the only way to have a lasting and successful business. That's why the companies who follow it are in business generation after generation. Servant leadership lasts, while self-serving leadership can only endure for a few years before self-destructing. The Golden Rule is also the best rule for living in personal relationships as well. Marriage and family problems fade away when people lovingly reach out to help each other by modeling the unselfish love of Jesus Christ.[1]

The message of the marble guides my coaching and counseling practice by keeping me mindful of serving and treating every person with great respect. When helping others, I have prayed to be tuned in to their needs and to be direct with the changes they may need to make to find greater success. God has used some wonderful people to help me along the path of personal growth, and I want to be responsible to help others along that same path. One of those people is Helen Kroner, a dear senior citizen who once shared with me this poem that she wrote. This message has great meaning, because it reflects my life mission. I honor her by spreading her vision of positive communication to others.

> One man awake can awaken another.
> And the second can awaken his next-door brother.
> And the three awake, can awaken the town,
> by turning the whole place upside down.
> And the many awake can make such a fuss
> that they finally awaken the rest of us.
> One man up, with dawn in his eyes, multiplies!

Passing Fear with Your P.B. List

Athletes constantly need to raise the bar in their thinking to a "can-do" mentality of breaking limits instead of living bound by them. Learn to pay close attention to what I call a "P.B.," which stands for "Personal Best." Keep track of how well you have done or where you may have struggled. Once you have identified your fears of success as well as your limitations of what you think you can't do, remember to keep track of your personal efforts to move beyond your limitations. Refer to the coaching self-tests in this book again and again. Use them to monitor your progress and growth. By using this method, you will see your "P.B." file of successes continue to stretch into page after page of "wins" that you would have missed because you would have been afraid to try. One of the things I do with my coaching clients is to review their progress from month to month in the different areas of life they are working on. We always end up pleased at the progress, which may have gone unnoticed without the success tracking reflected on their "P.B." list.

As long as coaches train their athletes to think about shattering records instead of being limited by them, records will be broken again and again. The same is true in business, health care, agriculture, industry, humanitarian agencies, filmmaking, or any one of the over eighteen thousand career fields listed in the *Directory of Occupational Titles* published by the U.S. Government. Records will be set, and records will be shattered. When you decide to move past your self-imposed limitations, records will fall.

Invisible Barriers Stop Success

Imagine traveling back in time six hundred years and looking down on the earth from a position in space. As you watched the great sailing vessels of the Renaissance period sail the Atlantic Ocean, you would notice something weird: As they set sail off the coast of Europe or Africa, they would go out a few hundred miles from the coast and then make a beeline back to the safety of the shoreline. Why wouldn't they just keep sailing on to the "new worlds" of the western hemisphere? Why not move on past the curvature of their little corner of the earth to visit the other side?

You know why: They were scared to death of an invisible barrier. Oddly, they weren't afraid to sail their fifty-foot ships out into a massive stretch of ocean, often battling with hurricane-strength storms in leaky wooden vessels. No radar, no instruments, no Coast Guard, no inflatable lifeboats, no midnight buffet on the Emerald Deck! These guys were seemingly fearless of the tremendous power of the ocean yet were immobilized by fear of an alleged limitation. Their seafaring fathers and grandfathers had passed on to them the idea that trying to cross the ocean was an unspeakable danger. It just couldn't be done.

What stopped civilization from moving forward toward new lands? The idea that one would fall off the edge of the earth of course! The invisible barrier served a good purpose: It kept everyone safe. Just stay close to home and enjoy whatever life you were given in Spain, Italy, France, England, Germany, Africa, the Middle East, or wherever you came from. Sail on the Mediterranean Sea or cruise on the English Channel, but stay away from the "dreaded edge" of the Atlantic. Learn to live with these nice countries as "all there is" and just be happy. Learn to be content with the hand that life dealt you and stick with what you got. Make do and just live with it. That's the philosophy that served as the barrier that kept thousands of people from attempting to cross the Atlantic.

Passion Breaks the Barrier

But Christopher Columbus didn't believe it. He refused to just "live with it." He saw the same limitations everyone else saw, but he spent all of his time trying to move beyond the barrier instead of being boxed in by it. His time, energy, and passions were focused on breaking the barriers instead of complaining about the limitations. He used his creative energy as author Katherine Mansfield centuries later advised: "Risk anything! Do the hardest thing on earth for you. Act for yourself." You know the rest of the story. Columbus hocked everything he had and made plans to cross the barrier. He was passionate, driven by his purpose.

Columbus must have heard the phrase "crazy man" continually. He was rejected, misunderstood, and criticized by everyone, including his own family, yet he kept pressing toward that centuries-old limitation. His passion led him from kingdom to kingdom to beg for financial backing to fund his "impossible" journey. While most people probably thought he was a nut, his personal belief in this journey took him to the Queen of Spain, who heard him out. (If you have ever gone from bank to bank trying to secure a loan for venture capital for your business plan, you know how Columbus must have felt.)

Chris tirelessly moved on toward his goal of finding financial backing. He let nothing get in his way of success. Bill Gates reflected on Columbus's remarkable insight to move beyond objections and obstacles with these words: "What if Columbus had been told, 'Chris, baby, don't go now. Wait until we've solved our number-one priorities: war and famine; poverty and crime; pollution and disease; illiteracy and racial hatred'?" Thankfully, nothing could stop this man. Yet how could he convince people to believe that the world is round when everyone "knew" that it was flat? Furthermore, how could he get someone to pay to prove he was right? Someone once joked that Columbus was the original politician, because he didn't know where he was going, didn't know where he was when he finally got there, and he did the whole project on other people's money!

Columbus made three trans-Atlantic journeys to the Caribbean from Spain. He charted and mapped out major ports in the Bahamas and on the Florida coast. In the process of exploring the mainland, he was struck with the tropical beauty of the state. What a sight those sailors must have seen! Pods of bottle-nosed dolphins, sea turtles, monster alligators, sailfish occasionally leaping into the sky—everything about their journey would have been new and exciting. Even in the 1500s people were going to Daytona, the world's most famous beach! The beauty and adventure of exploring a new country would have been the thrill of a lifetime! Those explorers lived these words of Helen Keller: "Life is a daring adventure or nothing at all!"

The Columbus Factor

Think about Columbus the man for a few minutes. What characteristics contributed to his successfully breaking through the "edge of the world" barrier to give everyone in Europe a chance at a new way of life?

Spiritual

Columbus had a strong faith in God. Tradition says that one of his driving forces to find a new trade route was to share the message of Christ with others and help to fulfill the Great Commission of sharing the gospel with the whole world. His personal diary records the many times on each voyage that he prayed to God for protection, guidance, and strength.

Financial

Columbus was not motivated by gold or greed, which sadly was the main motivation of some of the other explorers. He made three trips to the New World, which he claimed for his venture capitalist partner, Spain. Money wasn't his motivation and wasn't even a priority. In fact, he died penniless. His discovery made millions of dollars for Spain and opened up the door for the rest of the European countries to expand their territory and financial holdings as well. He missed out on making any reasonable financial return for the many years he invested in the biggest project of his lifetime. His family suffered with his absence, often years at a time, and then received no lasting financial support after his death. This was one of his greatest failures, because personal leadership and financial support are two of the primary tasks for men blessed with a family.

Career

Columbus was motivated by the thought of discovering a shorter trade route to India. This would have been a major boon to business, culture, and industry for all of Europe. Everyone, including Columbus, was thinking in the old paradigm of how to better connect to their world as they knew it. Improving the lives of those living in Europe, Africa, and Asia was his main focus. While he failed at discovering a new trade route, ironically he discovered a new world. He would never find a shortcut to India or China, but in failing to achieve his primary objective, he accomplished something greater. Pick up any dictionary or encyclopedia, and you will find Columbus. His career achievements are monumental, and he was one of the most influential men of his millennium.

Relationship

Networking was Columbus's hidden strength. Not only did he succeed in moving beyond the limitation of finding someone who would believe enough in his mission to give him venture capital, but he also found a crew adventuresome enough to outfit and sail three small ships on an uncharted journey. Columbus must have had amazing people skills to convince so many people to go along with his vision of what hadn't even yet been discovered. His social capital was a major reason for his success; his vision was much larger than he ever could have accomplished alone.

Would You Join the Crew?

Columbus was a success in many areas of life. He changed the world by moving beyond the current thinking to do things that had never been done. But if you were a skilled sailor with a stable life on the mainland, would you have signed up to sail with him?

- Would you have risked dying to prove the theory of a man whom you had never met?
- Would you have wanted to be a part of breaking a four-thousand-year-old tradition?
- What would you have said to your family as you departed, perhaps never to see them again?
- What would you have felt in the middle of the ocean with no land in sight?
- Would you have questioned if you were going to return home and be labeled a hero or be forever branded a nut?
- What would it have taken to get you onto the Niña, Pinta, or Santa Maria? (Money, the possibility of fame,

excitement of exploration, quest of a lifetime, or escape from a nagging spouse who would make any sea monsters that you might encounter seem tame?)

- Would you have moved boldly toward breaking the barriers, or would you have wanted to stay safely on the Mediterranean shore?

A New View of Possible

You know the name of Columbus today because he was able to move beyond barriers. He broke through the limitations of culture, cash flow, and cowardice. He had to overcome his own personal fears to be able to convince others. He had to see beyond the impossible by moving "Im" out of the way. "Im" is always in the path of possible. A success seeker moves around it. Study the interpretations below to discover a new view of the word *possible*; then apply it to change your life.

Impossible

Can't do it. Give up now. It cannot be done.

Im Possible

Im is in the way of possible. Im is blocking possible from happening.

I'm Possible

Yes! I can do this! I'm free to pursue my possibilities.

Now is your time to move to the "I'm Possible" stage. Are you ready for a breakthrough? Coaching you past these self-imposed mental barriers is the next important step on our adventure to the life you've always wanted. You have come a long way down the path of facing success fears by overcoming personal weakness. This part of your journey leads to another path, one that is steep and scary. The cliffs are going to sometimes block your view of success, but don't stop climbing. This is the part where you will move forward to tackle the most dangerous part of your personality.

Only the Strong Survive

Self-sabotage is the tendency to self-destruct over the hidden evils that lurk in the shadows of your soul. This darkness has held you down for too long, and it is time to bring the glowing light of success to those gloomy corners. As you boldly move forward in the darkness, each step will bring the light of a new way of thinking, blazing through the misty fog of your past failures and fears. This will be the most challenging part of your journey. Why? Because it takes a lot of courage to deal with these concealed dangers that have been blocking you from the successful life you have desired.

The next part of our journey may be difficult, but it's time to step on board the same vessel that Columbus used to reach his destination. This ship is named "mindset;" it alone has the strength to carry you beyond your fears to see the success on the other side.

Ready to challenge your fears? Ready to set sail to a new world of possibilities?

Then take a breath and step on board!

SEVEN

SELF-SABOTAGE—THE MOST DANGEROUS PART OF YOU

The hardest lesson in life to learn is which bridge to cross and which to burn.

—Jane Williams

Part of you is dangerous. Surprised? Are you shocked to learn that there is an element in the darkness of your soul that is bent on self-destruction? If you don't believe it, then just take a look at this week's newspaper to see which mega-star recently crashed and burned his or her career through sex, drugs, or alcohol. I hope that you have moved past the temptation of addiction, but I'm going to show you some hidden areas that are slowly destroying you by sucking the life out of you just as actively as heroin does. This weakness in your soul is dedicated to ruining any possibility that you may have for lasting and true success. Like the tape-recorded message in *Mission Impossible*, your vision of a better life could self-destruct in a puff of blue smoke.

Bridge Burning for a Better Life

Look into the mirror of your soul to begin to face this dangerous part of you, the part that lives in the darkness of your deepest fears and doubts. You may face some serious roadblocks that have hindered your family for generations. You may see shortages that leave you wondering how you could ever find the resources needed to solve the problems and move on. You will not only need to give up on some of your false beliefs, but you will have to burn the bridge leading back to them as well. Consider the wisdom of this phrase: "The hardest lesson in life to learn is which bridge to cross and which to burn." The challenge on this part of your journey to success is to move past the self-destructive behaviors that are killing your chances to experience a better life as well as possibly literally killing you.

It is equally important to burn the bridges that lead back to the old negative behaviors that have limited you in achieving a deeper level of success. Once you have the victory of overcoming these areas of personal weakness, you either must burn the bridge or live a lifetime of continual defeat. Why? Because when the stress of life increases, the dark side of doubts and fear always wants to run back over the bridge to self-destructive habits. One side of the bridge has life—the other side death. Choose life, and burn the bridges back to the way of defeat.

Missing Success because of Self-Sabotage

My friend Steve Brown tells a story about a guy who confused those choices. A bum, who obviously has seen more than his share of hard times, approaches a well-dressed gentleman on the street and says, "Hey, buddy, can you spare five bucks?" The well-dressed gentleman responds, "You're not going to spend it on liquor are you?" "No, sir, I don't drink," retorts the bum. "You're not going to throw it away in some crap game are you?" asks the gentleman. "No way, I don't gamble," answers the bum. "You wouldn't waste the money at a golf course for green fees, would you?" asks the man. "Never," says the bum; "I don't play golf." The man asks the bum if he would like to come home with him for a home-cooked meal. The bum eagerly accepts. While they are heading for the man's house, the bum's curiosity gets the best of him. "Isn't your wife going to be angry when she sees a guy like me at your table?" "Probably," says the man, "but it will be worth it. I want her to see what happens to a guy who doesn't drink, gamble, or play golf!"

Here's the application for you and I to follow: Too many times we look to other people as a reference point for our success. We compare our strengths to others' weaknesses to make ourselves feel better—but it doesn't work. If you are trying to fake your way to a successful life, it will fail, because that is just another form of deception, and self-deception always leads to self-destruction. We sabotage our lives in multiple and complex ways. Some are obvious, and others are much more difficult to spot. Think in terms of active self-destructive behaviors and then passive ones. When you are weak, you don't enjoy the level of success in life that you are capable of experiencing. My goal is to coach you beyond your self-imposed limitations and previous self-destructive behaviors. Let's get honest. Let's get real. Let's get going! Let's break through the barriers of your self-destructive tendencies.

Search Your Heart

Psychologist Gary Rosburg teaches a weekly meeting of Iowa businessmen about successful life application principles. One of the biblical principles he shares comes from an ancient Jewish king: "Keep your heart with all diligence, for out of it spring the issues of life" (Prov. 4:23 NKJV). History records that King Solomon was incredibly wealthy, powerful, and wise. His teaching is found in the Book of Proverbs. Even though it was written over three thousand years ago, it is still one of the best places to discover insight about why people do the things they do. Dr. Rosburg said that this principle changed his life and guided him as he coached businessmen at the crossroads of despair and destruction. His success in helping thousands of men find their way back to their core values is a testament to the power of this biblical principle and the importance of having a coach to walk with you on the journey so that you are not going through your problems alone. If you walk alone, you are likely to continue to repeat the same self-destructive cycle that has cost you too much already.

The Frozen Chosen

If you have ever gone to a school reunion, you have likely noticed two things. First, how old and overweight everyone besides you has gotten, and second, how some people are still talking about what they are going to do "some day." Some people call this group the "frozen chosen" because of their ability to remain emotionally stuck or "frozen" for decades! If you take the time to talk to them or, better yet, have kept in touch with them through the years, then you may have noticed that they are still struggling with the same problems they had in high school twenty-five years earlier! Something inside was frozen or stuck on the never-really-grow setting of their mind. Maybe this describes you. Here are some warning indicators that part of you is stuck on self-destruct:

- Have you been on a diet for years yet still are over-weight?
- Is your checkbook a disaster area of unmanaged debts?
- Are your relationships so dysfunctional that they are constantly sucking the life out of you?
- Do you bounce from job to job, often being fired because of "not being a team player" (read as "She has major personality problems")?
- Have you felt terribly misunderstood by family members who criticize and nag you about the same things over and over?
- Have your last ten years been your best decade ever, or have you gone from having minor problems to moving on to crisis events of biblical proportions?
- Are you sick and tired of being sick and tired?
- Do you ever wonder why you constantly do the same irresponsible things?

If any of these things is evident in your life, then you know that it is time to make a major adjustment to the way you are living. You may be stuck on a slow path of self-destruction. You may need what motivational guru Zig Ziglar calls a "check-up from the neck up," like going to a Jiffy Lube for your brain! We are usually pretty disciplined about getting our cars in for a three-thousand-mile oil change or a sixty-thousand-mile tune-up, yet we *never* seem to get away to work on the most important areas of life. When was the last time you had a crisis? Did you have the level of support you needed to manage that crisis, or were you up the creek without the proverbial paddle? Turn the question around if you are really brave: When was the last time you had a great time? When was the last time you had a deep-tissue massage or took time to enjoy a good book by the fire or to play a round of golf with friends? When was the last time you had more money than month?

Check Up on the Soul instead of the Scale

A check-up for the soul is one of the most valuable habits of the successful. A check-up on the way you have been thinking will help you to see instantly what is and isn't working well for you on your journey to a healthier way of life. Both are important, with the awareness of weakness being the more significant of the two. If you know what is weak, you can start to do something about it. If you don't, you will continue to have the same problems. Perhaps that is why so many people avoid this step to having the life they have always wanted. Honestly dealing with your own tendency to self-sabotage will not be easy. It's sort of like taking apart an eighteen-speed mountain bike and putting it back together; it's easy to tear apart but really hard to put back together again.

Self-sabotage happens all the time. People put themselves down, attack their core values, and do just about everything except wear a sign that says, "I'm programmed to fail; just watch me!" Just yesterday I was getting into an elevator, and as the door was closing, three young women squeezed in before the door closed. The last one tripped the electric eye that makes the door bounce back open, which apparently embarrassed her. She said, "Gosh, my butt is so big, no wonder it tripped the door." The odd thing is that this woman was petite. As the door reset, she proceeded to tell her equally skinny coworkers how she was always putting herself down for being fat. They all left the elevator chattering about how they were "so fat" and worried about their weight and not fitting into their clothes. I suspect that you can relate to this story, perhaps personally or with your daughter, sister, or friends.

Why are some women so preoccupied with their weight? The many possible explanations include, for example, the supermodel syndrome of feeling constant media pressure to be thin, comparisons with other women, secret eating disorders, and on and on. But the real root issue driving their behavior is the tendency to self-sabotage. The problem is inside and is caused by a mindset of failure. Whether you believe you are fat or a failure, you are creating many of your own problems. Therefore, you must take responsibility for dealing with those problems. Facing and moving beyond your fears will be a challenge, but it is essential to climb up to a new level of success. The next strategy for you to master is a life-changing formula to understand and implement as you deal with your tendency to self-sabotage.

$$C = C$$

Choices equal your *Consequences*

If you pay more attention to your choices, you will likely see dramatic results in your consequences. It happens quickly, and the results will excite you. $C = C$ works! The decisions you and I make are responsible for many, if not most, of the pleasures or problems we ultimately receive. Let me show you what I mean by contrasting different choices in various areas of life. Note which category best illustrates your typical response to the events of your daily life.

Eat right, exercise, get enough sleep, and stay hydrated = Feel great	Eat junk, become a bleary-eyed, dehydrated couch potato = Feel terrible
Love, accept, forgive, call, e-mail, and pray for others = Build relationships	Ignore people, be moody, spiteful, and resentful of others = Be isolated and lonely
Work, save, invest, diversify portfolio, delay gratification, take a long view = Wealth	Spend, waste, be idle, seek immediate gratification, take a temporary view = Poverty
Face issues, deal with emotions, list options, talk through options = Find solutions	Avoid issues, stuff emotions, overlook options, silently suffer = Problems grow
Read, study, imagine, dream, plan, prepare, connect with ideas = Win at life	Lounge, ignore, numbly watch, fantasize, resent others, complain = Lose at life

If most of your life is spent on the right-hand scenarios, you are cheating yourself out of a lot of success. Deal with your problems now and don't blame them on your parents. Blame-shifting is just another ugly form of self-sabotage.

Why Is Life So Unfair?

After guiding thousands of people through crisis events, I can tell you that sometimes life isn't very fun. Sometimes you have to make sacrifices that are remarkably painful. Sometimes life is about just hanging on in the tough times with the hope that there will be good times ahead. Sometimes life is a dark and difficult journey that would be impossible if it weren't for God's kindness and mercy to help us deal with the pressures and problems. As a counselor, I have walked through the valley of doubt and discouragement with thousands of people. At the breaking point, when people want to question God with "Why do you allow life to be so hard and unfair?" I have learned to listen and let them vent for a while. Then I quietly remind them that God isn't life. God is bigger than life. He is above life. He created life, and sometimes it just doesn't make any sense to us at the time that we are living it. Eventually you can trace some lesson or application, but it still may not seem fair. Life is more than enjoyment, and it is more than endurance. Life is about living well. Wise choices in good and bad times will make you a healthier individual.

Hard Things Can Be Good Things

Action film hero Bruce Willis revealed that he had learned that hard things can be good things when he commented on how poorly he had managed his opportunities in life. He shared his insights on being self-destructive: "I didn't deal very well with being famous. Now I've given up trying to correct the world's attitude of who I am as a man. People don't want to know that I feel like a regular guy. Every man knows there's a line in life between good and bad. Unless you are a sociopath, you know where that line is. Huge chunks of my time have been on the dark side." Willis made these comments after his failed marriage to actress Demi Moore and the sudden cancer and death of his forty-two-year-old brother, Robert. Willis has had to deal with some painful losses, as well as bad choices, just like the rest of us. He disclosed that he had partied too much while working as a bartender in New York, hoping to "make it big" as an actor. He said, "I drank a lot. I took drugs. Yeah, in my checkered past, I did bad things. I no longer do them. I don't judge anyone who succumbs to an addiction, because life's a scary, hard thing, but I saw addiction for what it was. I had goals. There were more important things."[1]

I admire the courage that Bruce Willis has shown to publicly face his weaknesses and tendency to self-destruct. I admire how he left a secure job with the DuPont chemical plant in New Jersey to move to New York and pursue his dream of acting when he was only eighteen years old. His dad told him that he was making a big mistake to leave the security of DuPont to chase his dream, but he left anyway. It was a hard thing but a good thing.

Willis went on to win the leading role in the television series *Moonlighting* and then starred in hit movies like *Die Hard*, *Pulp Fiction*, and *Hart's War*. Willis now commands a fee of $20 million per picture and is one of Hollywood's most bankable stars. He has faced some of the demons that led to his self-destructive behavior and has come up with this conclusion: "I look at my life now, and I know I've been blessed by God. My life's a work in progress. All I've learned in forty-six years is that I want to live my life as a good man and a good father. I'm still trying to figure it out, but I believe the best is yet to come."[2] Do you see the growth and maturity in his answer? Sadly, it took painful choices for him to come to some of his insights. Perhaps you and I can learn from his mistakes and not make those same self-destructive choices.

I want you to feel good! I want you to experience contentment and deep satisfaction. I want you to be stronger emotionally than you ever have been. But you will need to deal with some key issues in order to accomplish this new level of personal power and contentment. Then, no matter what the circumstances, you can become increasingly successful. Learning how to manage life and make good choices is the key to dealing with the ebb and flow of the positive and negative events of life.

As Winston Churchill said, "This is no time for ease and comfort. It is the time to dare and endure." Yes, difficulties and stress will abound, but a successful person faces and deals with problems rather than avoiding them or lying about how things are "just fine." Learn to laugh at the insignificant "spilled milk" experiences of life instead of losing your cool over them. Laughing sometimes will turn your crisis event into a learning event as you accept that life doesn't always turn out the way you planned. Accept the fact that some days you're the statue and on other days you're the pigeon.

Dreams or Nightmares?

Take time to search your heart and uncover any hidden areas of weakness limiting you from the life you desire to live. There are two categories to consider: active and passive self-destructive behavior. Either functions as a roadblock to your dreams and very well may show up as the nightmare in your world. Since you might be your own worst enemy at times, you will need to do whatever it takes to honestly identify the area of weakness. This may mean that you go to a trusted friend or pastor to ask for insight and counsel. It may mean that you ask your mother! If you want to achieve your dreams, then one of the most difficult parts of the journey begins here and now.

Either type of self-destructive behavior will lead to a nightmare of a life, so begin now to admit to any weakness holding you back. Check off the issues that apply to your life either today or from your past. This will show the dangerous areas of weakness that you may have and, more significantly, the key issues you need to work on.

Active Self-destructive Behavior

____ alcoholism

____ drug addiction (prescription or illegal)

____ sex addiction

____ gambling addiction

____ food addiction

____ rage (explosive disorders)

Any of these behaviors can ruin your life. People usually struggle in one area. If their proclivity is toward drugs, they may not struggle with food addiction at all. If they are addicted to sex, they may have no problem with alcohol. Impulsive rage can be more dangerous than any of the others since it can lead to loss of control and homicide. The stronger your addictions, the more your hopes for a better life are buried underneath the consequences of your reckless and irresponsible behavior. It is time to stop and get help. It is time to change. Someone once said that "a bend in the road is not the end of the road unless you fail to make the turn."

If you have any of these self-destructive behaviors, you probably need to talk with a professional therapist as well as your personal physician as soon as possible. These problems are bigger than you and will destroy your dreams. Biochemical or medical problems may have led to long-term addictions that require the care of a medical or psychological professional. Deal with them, and you can change. Start now!

Passive self-destructive behaviors are equally dangerous roadblocks to living out your dreams, yet they are so common that people joke about having them! They may be the hidden reason you are not experiencing the level of success in life that you are capable of achieving. Identify the passive self-destructive behaviors that may be standing between you and your dreams.

Passive Self-destructive Behaviors

____ media addiction
(absurd amounts of time invested in music, sports, TV, or the Internet)

____ procrastination

(never finishing important tasks or not starting any major task)

____ irresponsible behavior

(driving, spending, or living recklessly; cheating, shoplifting, or lying)

____ immaturity

(petty, jealous, moody, and self-absorbed behaviors; throwing tantrums)

____ perfectionism

(the compulsive need to only do things the way you want them done)

____ critical whining

(chronic complaining and attacking of others; leads to resentment)

____ workaholism

(totally consumed with being busy; can apply to religion as well)

____ escapism

(compulsively using hobbies, trips, pets, or yard work to avoid facing reality)

____ materialism

(saving money to spend on certain items, which are then idolized)

____ consumerism

(irresponsibly spending money on things that are often discarded)

____ infatuation

(romantic or lustful daydreams that may lead to sex addiction)

____ past abuse and trauma

(unresolved psychological issues and problems of your past)

You Are Responsible for Your Future

Next on our journey, we will discover the success formula that will take you past your fears. But first you have to deal with any trait that keeps you from being your best. Like listening to the radio for traffic reports during rush hour, if you know where the roadblocks, detours, and wrecks are, you can find a better route to the places you want to go. If you just keep driving on the highway without a plan, there is no telling where you will end up or how long it will take you to get there. Noted relationship psychologist Dr. Phil McGraw says, "Life is a journey; as with any other trip, if you don't have a map, a plan, and a timetable, you will get lost. On the other hand, with a well-thought-out, realistic, serious plan, you will be amazed at what can happen." Your lists of active and passive self-destructive behaviors will be central to your moving toward greater success.

Dealing with self-sabotage begins with the awareness that you alone are ultimately responsible for your future. A little boy once was asked by a visitor to his town where a particular road would take him. The little guy smiled and said, "Mister, that road will take you anywhere in the world you want to go!" Likewise, we can go forward in any direction if we deal with our personal roadblocks.

Moving Beyond "Lucy" Living

The classic *I Love Lucy* episodes were funny because of the cycle of predicaments Lucy would get into. She would always end up in a harebrained scheme. The audience could see it coming. Ethel could. Fred could. Ricky could. But Lucy never did. We all laughed because we could relate to how the plot always led to some disastrous result. Or perhaps we laughed because we had done many of the same things. I wish I had never burned the toast, or been starstruck by some celebrity, or misrepresented myself to look good to someone I had grown up around, or took part in some scheme to get rich quick, or ignored the good advice of my friends and family. Perhaps my screwups weren't as catastrophic as lighting my nose on fire, or having to stuff chocolates into my shirt, or being locked in a flooding shower stall or freezing meat locker. But some of my worst choices were pretty close to Lucy's hair-brained schemes, and I'll bet yours were too!

The good news is that there wasn't a camera crew to record your screwups for the world to see, and they weren't featured on CNN. The bad news is that your brain made a DVD of the entire tragic event—multiple camera angles, Dolby sound effects, close-up reaction shots, and slow-mo replays of your worst disasters. It's all there in Technicolor on the IMAX screen in your mind. We tend to keep those negative images for a lifetime and refer back to them to justify why we aren't more successful. You have created many of the barriers to your own success. If you live behind those barriers, you will miss having success over yourself. Success over self means many things:

It's about moving past your past.
It's about rewriting your life script.

It's about changing the ending.

It's about moving on.

It's about living well.

It's good.

Oh yes, here are some other things you need to know about success over self:

It's rare.

It's real.

It's valuable.

It's obtainable.

It's worth the effort.

It's waiting on you.

Some big barriers stand in your way—your past mistakes, the negative influence of others, your own mental picture of success, and the difficulties of our culture. Besides, success is harder to capture than failure—it takes great effort.

Choose Your Chair Carefully

A wonderful story from the great tenor Luciano Pavarotti illustrates the importance of making a choice, a choice to move beyond the mistakes of the past and beyond fears, doubts, and insecurities. Furthermore, it tells about the victorious choice to become the best.

When I was a boy, my father, a baker, introduced me to the wonders of song. He urged me to work very hard to develop my voice. Arrigo Pola, a professional tenor in my hometown of Modena, Italy, took me as a pupil. I also enrolled in a teachers college.

On graduating, I asked my father, "Shall I be a teacher or a singer?"

"Luciano," my father replied, "if you try to sit on two chairs, you will fall between them. For life, you must choose one chair."

I chose one. It took seven years of study and frustration before I made my first professional appearance. It took another seven to reach the Metropolitan Opera. And now I think whether it's laying bricks, writing a book—whatever we choose—we should give ourselves to it. Commitment, that's the key. Choose one chair.

Choices lead to consequences. That's what you and I have learned on this part of our journey. Pavarotti made a good choice. And so did those that went on to become teachers. The payoff for choosing well is huge; your life will be a thousand times better if you cross the bridge and move toward your goals. The reward for choosing poorly could be catastrophic, because the consequences of running back over the bridge to self-destructive tendencies will lead to ruin.

If you decide to let this be your time to move beyond self-destructive tendencies, your future will be so bright you'll need sunglasses! If not, your future will be put on hold, and your options will grow increasingly dim as the darkness of failure begins to cover your dreams.

It's time for you to choose your chair. Choose wisely. And when you have made a choice, we'll move past your success fears to master the success formula.

EIGHT

Secret #4

DEVELOPING PERSONAL
DISCIPLINE TO DISCOVER
YOUR DESTINY

The measure of success is not whether you have a tough
problem to deal with, but whether it's the same problem
you had last year.

—John Foster Dulles

It seems the whole world eventually comes to central
Florida—families, grandparents, honeymooners, businesspeople, international tour groups, professional athletes, and even NASA rocket scientists. Orlando has become
one of the most visited cities on the planet, with almost a

million guests per week. Why? What is it about the center part of the Florida peninsula that draws people from around the globe? The answer may surprise you.

The Reason the World Comes to Visit

Some people come here to be amused, and some come to recreate. Notice that neither group visits just to goof off; there is a tremendous difference. Look at the words *amuse* and *recreate* to learn a powerful life-changing lesson. This concept is the foundation for the next success secret.

Amusement parks are designed to entertain. But what does amusement really mean? *Amuse* means the opposite of *muse*, which means to think deeply about something. So amusement is the process of not thinking deeply, but rather superficially, about a subject. Literally it means to shut off your mind and not think about things while you are being entertained. Is that bad? No, it's like popcorn at a movie; the enjoyable taste is part of the total entertainment experience, but you can't make a meal out of it.

Some people visit to shut off their brains and not think about the deepest part of their lives. So, for a little while, they focus on having fun by riding roller coasters, shaking hands with teenagers dressed up as their favorite cartoon characters, and getting squirted with water by animatronic dinosaurs. These tourists leave after a few days with less money and very little to show for what they spent besides their snapshots and bags of souvenirs.

Others come to be challenged at the deepest level and are mentally refreshed for years every time they hear the words "world's most famous beach," "space shuttle lift-off," or "Disney World." That's recreation. How did they do it? What was the secret that made such a difference?

The Difference Is the Dash

Look at the word *recreate* in a new way, and it will change your life. Just add a hyphen—*re-create*. Proper recreation will re-create energy and focus. People do that in a variety of ways: golfing, surfing, indoor rock climbing, swimming, fishing, water skiing, wake-boarding, hiking, walking, sunbathing, scuba-diving, weight-lifting, go-carting, hitting balls at the batting cage, biking, throwing a Frisbee in the park, skating, canoeing, snorkeling, four-wheeling, playing tennis, playing music, and of course, the classic activity that you may think of when you think about central Florida, walking with their children or grandchildren through a theme park or the Kennedy Space Center and seeing the wonder and excitement on their young faces!

Re-creation often involves others—like playing on a company softball team or bowling league. And sometimes it involves the energizing leadership aspect of coaching or helping with activities like T-ball, gymnastics, football, basketball, baseball, soccer, swimming, diving, wrestling, track, aerobics, cheerleading, or martial arts.

You can hurriedly gulp down a Starbucks Carmel Macchiato or sit with a dear friend and slowly enjoy one. The first approach is a novel way to spend four bucks on hot, stimulating liquid, while the other approach provides an opportunity to connect and catch up with someone you care about. Maybe the reason Starbucks is so successful is that they sell experiences instead of just coffee. Almost any activity can draw you and friends or family closer, or it can be just another way to spend money.

Last summer my son Garrett and I visited Wrigley Field in Chicago to watch a Cubs game. It was his first major league game, so we did the total entertainment package! We shared popcorn, cotton candy, peanuts, Cracker Jacks, and a large lemon ice. We bought stuffed animals, T-shirts, and ball caps to show our support for one of Chicago's favorite teams. We waved big foam fingers on the first-base line with hopes of watching Sammy Sosa hit a home run over the ivy-covered wall in center field. We had a ball! Even though the Cubbies lost the game, we had a wonderful time that we will forever remember and enjoy. I smile every time I think about it.

Experience the Power of Positive Energy

Re-creation is at work when we have a positive experience and then relive it again and again. It's a gift we will forever treasure, because the memories of recreation with people we love will last a lifetime. Have you noticed how the elderly can remember positive events from their youth? Sometimes these senior citizens can't remember who the president is, but they can remember playing in the barn with their cousins or riding a pony at the state fair when they were kids. They can remember events seventy years old better than what happened last week. How do they do it? Simple. Re-creation is so powerful that it carves out a special place in our memory. Learning this skill will speed you along your journey to lasting success.

Protect Your Re-creation Experiences

Often people will think back to a special date or the beginning of a relationship and enjoy the chemistry and excitement of feeling in love and then immediately "steal" that emotion by remembering that the relationship ended poorly. Stop that! You can remember the positive or the negative. You get to

---

Try it!

Take a minute to experience true re-creation of your energy. Set this book aside for a moment, sit back in your chair, and take a deep breath. Slowly let it out. Now think about a fun event or experience that you have participated in within the last ten years.

What did you do?
With whom did you share the experience?
What made it such a good time?

You may need to close your eyes to relive the fun of true re-creation. Maybe it was eating a special dinner at a great restaurant, or watching the wonder of a child's eyes on Christmas morning, or singing hymns with a loved one who was nearing death after a long life of blessings, or boating with friends and enjoying subs and sodas on a remote part of the river, or sitting on the roof of a friend's motor home cheering on your favorite NASCAR driver at the Daytona 500, or reading stories to your little girl at bedtime. This is true re-creation of energy, which comes from completely experiencing life instead of just watching others have the experience. This is the beginning of really living and being grateful to God for the gift of being alive.

---

choose! Remember that we are rewriting your life script, so instead of always replaying the bad ending of things in your mind, enjoy the beginnings. Think back to the fun, the wonder and the joy of each experience or consider the difficult times and be grateful for those as well. The failures and frustrations of life taught you and shaped you into a better person. Count your blessings instead of your problems. Learn to savor each moment. A television credit card commercial shows a couple having a special picnic on an isolated stretch of beach and then tells how much the picnic cost. The ad ends with the word "Priceless," because the money was shown to be a good trade for the powerful experience.

Dr. Jim Henry, the pastor of the church where our family worships, taught me a wonderful lesson when my children were very young. He advised, "Spend your money on experiences for your children and not just on toys." I have appreciated his advice through the years of watching my kids grow. Oh, they have had their share of toys (which they eventually have outgrown and put in a yard sale), but they also have had their share of fun experiences. This is a great lesson reflecting the concept of re-creation as a core value for family activities instead of only investing in the short-term amusement of trendy video games or toys or attending a popular movie. Can you remember the gifts you received on past holidays or birthdays? Can you even remember last year's gift? And if you could actually remember what you received on your eighth birthday, do you still have it? Does it still bring excitement and joy? I suspect that you couldn't even remember, but if I asked you about a special childhood memory, your face would light up as you described building a model car with your dad or making crafts with your grandmother.

The Best Part Is the People

Can you still spend time, energy, and money to attend professional sporting events without feeling guilty? Absolutely! Just remember the best part of attending professional sporting events is the people with whom you go. To re-create some excitement by using amusement, join with a friend to cohost a bowl game party. The secret is to focus more on the people attending the party than on who wins the championship. Everyone has a better time when they connect with people instead of watching another game on TV. Besides, can you even remember who won the Super Bowl seven years ago? Champions change every year, while friendships go on and on.

Are You Living Life or Watching It?

One group is watching life while the other is actively living it. Some guys watch as much as thirty-five hours a week of ESPN sports on TV. People who spend that much time watching sports are doing the same thing as others who watch sitcoms, soaps, or movies. They are being amused—no more, no less.

Now contrast watching sports with playing sports, which involves tremendous activity and sweat. Those playing are having the time of their lives by pushing themselves to a new level of exertion and competition. The others are quietly watching a satellite or video-taped episode of someone else on the field playing their hearts out. Here are some of the differences between these common activities.

Amusement	Recreation
Watching	Doing
Leisure (no sweating)	Active (sweating)
No discipline required	Discipline required
No health benefit	Some health benefit
Isolation (mostly alone)	Social connection with others
No teamwork required	Teamwork required
Tendency to self-focus	Tendency to focus on others
Connect to media image	Connect to real people
Empty feeling afterward	Energizing feeling afterward

Recreation is doing something with others and creating an experience that results in more value for you and those with whom you share it. Recreation keeps you young at heart and is usually good for your heart. Amusement tends to shut off your brain and body, which can lead to health problems associated with a sedentary lifestyle.

Does this mean that you should never watch a game on TV? No. It means that you have to get honest with the real reasons behind your behavior. Understand what motivates you to do things, especially any activity that might stand in the way of a more successful life. Even seemingly innocent things like watching football or ice-skating could become a roadblock. Leonardo da Vinci was likely thinking through a similar issue when he said, "Just as iron rusts from disuse, so does inaction spoil the intellect." Ask yourself, "Does this activity help me have a more successful life?" Sometimes it's hard to tell, so here's the balancing formula to protect recreation while still taking advantage of the benefits of amusement: Balance the use of media (watching life) with life experiences (living life).

Learn to be honest with the real reasons behind why you do things. If you want to relax by watching a sailing regatta, good; enjoy it! Make some popcorn. Light an aromatherapy candle. Stretch out on the couch. Take a mental break. All of these things help you because they can soothe your soul. But if you end up agitated that the wrong crew won or you spend three hours surfing through channels looking for something else to watch to escape the pressures of your life, then you missed the benefit those three hours could have given you. You wasted your time. And when you waste time, you're wasting life.

Get Creative with Amusement to Get Energy

Just yesterday I heard a local radio DJ talking about how she had gotten a new satellite TV system. She raved about how it had become the best part of her life. At first I thought it was an advertisement for the satellite company, but then I could tell that she was for real. She found a secret strength from media. How? By watching home and garden shows for relaxation. She found a calming benefit from entertainment, which is a positive way to use amusement in our busy lives. She soothed away stress by watching someone instruct her in a favorite activity. I suspect that she will later go out and practice those home-improvement techniques, illustrating the balancing formula of watching life with living it.

Just this week I felt like the most blessed man on the planet while ice-skating with my wife Sheila and children Heidi and Garrett. We were gliding along with the sound of the oldies tune "Play That Funky Music White Boy" in the background.

Does life get any better than that? True, my ankles are still sore, but who cares? We were re-creating way more energy than if we had been home being amused by watching ice-skating on television. Furthermore, I was able to educate them about a piece of American musical history called "The '70s." The positive memory of our time together lives on for each of us and always will. Amusement is good, but when it leads to the energy of re-creation, it's even better.

Surfing or Searching?

The problem with channel surfing is that surfers often don't know what they are hunting for, so they will never find it! I suspect that many TV surfers are searching for relief from stress. They are longing for a way to escape the pressure of overwhelming problems in their lives. They are looking for peace. They are searching for a way to find rest for their tired hearts and minds, and they are missing the wisdom of these words from Mark Twain: "What a robust people, what a nation of thinkers we might be, if we would only lay ourselves on the shelf occasionally and renew our edges."

Searching for relief from stress can be accomplished in many ways. You can be a media watcher of amusing things, or you can discover the hidden energy available from re-creation. If your goal is to support your favorite team, or to see whom Erica is marrying this week, or to find out which country declared war, or to unwind and catch a few laughs from a sitcom, okay. It's your time, and you can spend it any way you like. However, you can spend hundreds of hours watching other people have fun and end up feeling really empty. Perhaps there is a more beneficial use of that time. Imagine spending time doing things you enjoy and finding times of solitude and quiet rest. You have twelve months per year to spend on amusement or re-creation on your journey to a more successful life. Spend them wisely. As Charles Darwin said, "Anyone who dares waste one hour of life has not discovered the value of life." Activity that adds value, power, and passion for living is a key to a life of greater success and meaning.

Resentment or Refreshment?

There are two approaches to finding success. One approach leads to refreshment, while the other can often lead to resentment. Why? Because when the dust begins to settle after the event, the "amusement only" crowd may feel cheated over what they got for their money! You have seen this after an event and just didn't know what it was called. You even may have been sucked into the vacuum of postevent distress. It looks like this: You go to a big concert, you are swaying with the crowd, and everybody is feeling good! You are feeling like you are "one" with ten thousand of your fellow concert-goers! Then, "bam," just that fast, it's over! You now feel bad. You feel lonely, like you just lost ten thousand new friends. So what's the solution? Simple: Buy a T-shirt and CD to relive the experience. If your music and T-shirt help you to re-create the energy, you spent your money wisely. If you were just feeling empty and lonely, you wasted your money. You may only listen to the CD halfway through and spill a milkshake on the T-shirt and end up donating it to charity. When you understand this principle, you will likely make a strategic change to guide your *viewing* habits into *doing* habits!

I am coaching you to become a success seeker, a person who is dedicated to dealing with himself or herself first, before blaming others, rationalizing, justifying, or worse, wanting others to "fix" their problems for them. To become successful is to become focused on your goals and live a disciplined life to accomplish those goals. I heard a story once about an irresponsible young man that illustrates what happens if you miss this secret of lasting success.

The college-aged son of a middle-aged couple decided to communicate some bad news to his parents in a rather creative way. He sent an email to his mother that laid out his bleak situation.

"Failed all my classes.
Bank account is $1,500 overdrawn.
Girlfriend is pregnant.
PREPARE POP!"

He received back this email reply from his mother.

"POP PREPARED.
PREPARE YOURSELF!"

Are you prepared? Remember, a successful life is your responsibility, and no one else's. It is not the responsibility of your parents, best friend, marriage partner, boss, or government to hand you a good life. It is yours and yours alone. This secret will help transform your thinking, because it is directly linked to the power of your own potential. Are you ready to learn the next secret of a better life? Even more important, are you ready to begin living it? Will you take ownership to apply this truth? If so, here it is:

 The fourth success secret is to develop personal discipline to discover your destiny.

Lasting success is available, but it waits on you to show up and claim it. You have to keep growing and developing. You have to desire it and work at it. You and I have a responsibility to live out the destiny of a better life. Growing into the man or woman you were designed to be is one of the most important things you can do today. It means that you will be reading books, listening to tapes or CDs, and partnering with people who can help you on your journey to lasting success. It means that you will take the responsibility to face some issues and develop a daily discipline for living better. It means that you are going to aggressively deal with issues to move beyond the roadblocks that have held you back from the life you have desired. Your life isn't a dress rehearsal, and it's time to live like you are completely alive, celebrating the blessings you have been given by God.

You Are the Lucky One!

I received one of those letters in the mail recently that said, "You may be a winner!" You know what I did? I tossed it. I knew better. How? Simple: I have opened dozens of those through the years and spent hours of my life (hours that I will never get back) looking through all of the wonderful things I could win if I became the lucky one. Sadly, I have wasted too much time dreaming about how someone, somewhere, sometime might show up at my door and give me the million-dollar prize.

You, however, are already the lucky one. You have the winning ticket right now. You have what it takes to claim the prize. Here's what I mean: You can achieve more in life than what you currently have accomplished. You can find more fulfillment than you previously thought possible in every single aspect of your life. You—not some CPA in another city who is going to randomly pull your name out of the hat—control the destiny and timing of much of that success. The odds of winning a major sweepstakes are astronomically slim, but your odds of taking the initiative to live a more successful life is a sure bet. But you cannot experience this success if you don't have a disciplined plan of personal development.

Responsibility to Little Things Brings Big Success

You will need to learn some new skills and apply some new insights to make disciplined personal development happen and to set a new course to capture your destiny. You will be experiencing the life that few people ever know, because you are taking ownership to do the things that successful people do. Someone once said, "There is a close connection between getting up in the world and getting up in the morning." The daily discipline of getting up every day leads to a personal philosophy like this:

Successful people do hard things today that others really don't want to do and sometimes never will do. They do this so that they can do huge things tomorrow that others will never have a chance to do. Successful people take the responsibility to build a great life.

Charles Wang, founder, chairman, and CEO of Computer Associates, said, "I don't think success is a place or a definition, I think it's a direction. It's very important to look at how you're living your life—and it should be pointed in the right direction." So ask yourself if you are living the kind of life that leads to the places you want to go. Have you set up your plan, and more important, are you working that plan? Are you moving toward a better life? Are you having fun on the journey? I hope so!

Fast forward your life. Hit a button in your brain and consider what your world will look like in ten or twenty years. Do you see a successful life of being healthy, surrounded by those you care about and who love you in return? Or do you see a bitter and lonely old person, much like Scrooge in Charles Dickens's *A Christmas Carol*? I hope that you are maximizing your potential in key areas, because focused growth will take you to a new level of success. Personal growth will not only give you a more successful life but will protect you as well. If you are growing, you are protected from more problems than you can imagine, because many of the self-destructive behaviors we looked at in the last chapter are intensified when you stop growing. If you stop growing and then become self-absorbed with your doubts or get side-tracked from what you believe, you may end up with a ruined life.

Paradigm Shift—From Disappointment to Delight

People who achieve and hold on to lasting success follow a formula, as do the ones who fail to experience a better life. See which formula applies to you.

Distractions, dead ends, and detours lead to disaster—
a life filled with disappointment!

Discipline, development, and direction lead to destiny—
a life filled with delight!

If you are feeling somewhat stressed at this point, perhaps it is because you are becoming aware of some missing pieces of a balanced life. It may be that you are getting honest about some key areas that have needed attention for a long time. You may also be thinking of your children, corporate team, or loved ones. Are they balanced? Are they focused? Are they going to achieve lasting success by living out healthy choices? Could it be too late for you or someone you care about? No. It's never too late. That's the good news of this book. Listen to these wise words from George Eliot about living out potential: "It is never too late to be what you might have been."

So, if you could paint a successful future for yourself or a loved one, what would it look like? Would you own your own business, have a large family and loving marriage partner, and possess a positive cash flow? Would you include how well you were using your potential? To measure success by what you are doing with what you have to work with is honest because it measures potential. Some people don't have a lot of skills but work at 110 percent all the time. Others look like they have a good life but use only 35 percent of their skill set. Which one is the true success? Which one is happiest? Probably the person who is working with every bit of his or her potential. Which one is bored, unfulfilled, and apt to create many self-destructive behaviors to avoid those unpleasant feelings? Likely the one who is not living out his or her potential. Lack of personal development can destroy you, your family, or your team.

Be aware that not everyone will want you to improve and succeed. Watch out for people who want to stay in their dead-end lives. They are undisciplined people who enjoy using distractions to avoid being responsible for managing the details of their lives. As you begin to change, they might try to "throw you under the bus" instead of praising your accomplishments and helping you onto the bus to success. Learn to identify and move beyond that kind of petty person and take the initiative to deal responsibly with your own life. As you take ownership to live out your potential, you will enjoy the ride with others who have learned this secret. Leaving the losers behind is part of what it takes to move to a new level of success. My friend Billy Wright told me a sad story about an elderly friend who had given up on success because of his fears. He said, "I am more afraid of living than I am of just dying in the nursing home. I would rather face pity than have to deal with my purpose." How sad, yet how common it is to see individuals that missed the fourth secret of a more successful life.

A success seeker is committed to personal growth as a way to add value to others and help them live at a higher level and never take advantage of anyone. They do the hard work of personal discipline and growth. They share their insights with other travelers on this journey to a better life. They know that success in life doesn't come from one's age, IQ, bank account, career, family reputation, education, or physical health. Success is a way of life that is a reflection of one's personal and professional values and priorities.

If you want to experience lasting success, you will have to discipline yourself daily to practice skills that will drive you closer to your lifetime destiny. Life is moving on, and life is keeping score on your ability to build up to your potential. One day the buzzer will sound on the time clock of life signaling that you are out of time. How well you finish the game will be in direct proportion to your ability to honestly confront your personal weaknesses and build up to a new level of strength. You can do it, but you must begin right now.

The following autobiography is a powerful illustration of overcoming personal weakness to move forward to a life of greater success and meaning. It is one of the best stories I have heard relating to living out the fourth principle of lasting success.

An Autobiography in Five Chapters
Author Unknown

Chapter 1
I walk down the street.
There is a deep hole in the sidewalk.
I fall in.
I am lost. I am helpless.
It isn't my fault.
It takes forever to find a way out.

Chapter 2
I walk down the same street.
There is a deep hole in the sidewalk.
I pretend I don't see it.

I fall in again.
I can't believe I am in this same place.
But it isn't my fault.
It still takes a long time to get out.

Chapter 3
I walk down the same street.
There is a deep hole in the sidewalk.
I see it is there.
I fall in. It's a habit. But my eyes are open.
I know where I am.
It is my fault.
I get out immediately.

Chapter 4
I walk down the same street.
There is a deep hole in the sidewalk.
I walk around it.

Chapter 5
I walk down a different street.

You have faced fears, doubts, and insecurities and are moving beyond your fears of success. So now it's time to do a quick check on your progress toward the life you have desired. Ask yourself the following questions.

Am I disciplined to live out a daily routine that guarantees more success?

Am I maturing into a responsible person?

Am I ready to face my destiny?

Let's move on to the third part of our journey together, the success formula, where you will learn to achieve greater success in key areas of your life.

PART 3

THE SUCCESS FORMULA

If one advances confidently in the direction of his dreams and endeavors to live the life which he has imagined, he will meet with success unexpected in common hours. He will pass an invisible boundary; new universal and more liberal laws will begin to establish themselves around and within him; and he will live with the licenses of a higher order of being.

—Henry David Thoreau

NINE

Secret #5

BELIEF—FINDING YOUR HIDDEN SOURCE OF INNER STRENGTH

Belief is the knowledge that we can do something. It's the inner feeling that what we undertake, we can accomplish. For the most part, all of us have the ability to look at something and know whether or not we can do it. So, in belief there is power; our eyes are opened; our opportunities become plain; our visions become realities.

—John Maxwell

It was a quiet Tuesday morning during the last days of summer in 2001. I was coaching a young leader when my office administrator told me the grim news: A commercial jet had crashed into one of the towers of the World Trade Center in New York. During the next few minutes we watched the news live on NBC as another jumbo jet slammed into the remaining tower. Then within the half-hour another jet hit the Pentagon and another crashed in a Pennsylvania field. It seemed as if the country was in complete chaos, under attack from an unknown enemy. You already know the date.

September 11, 2001

You will always remember how you felt as you heard the news that America had been attacked. (In fact, you may be feeling it again right now.) September 11 marked the death of innocence and the end of an era of peace and safety. Ted Koppel summarized it by saying, "Nothing will ever be the same again." We would travel differently, manage our money and resources differently, and not trust much of anything or anyone the same ever again. The concepts of multiculturalism and open tolerance of foreigners would vanish in the dust of those destroyed buildings. The hopes and dreams of a safe country, free from the threat of evil, ended that day.

We were forced to face some terrible images—the second plane exploding into Tower Two, people leaping to their deaths from the tops of the blazing towers, and then the two buildings collapsing to the ground 110 stories below. Thousands of people were buried in the dust and rubble of the shattered World Trade Center complex. The FAA ceased every flight in the United States, and President George Bush was taken to hidden locations aboard Air Force One in an attempt to avoid being the victim of yet another terrorist attack. The stock market crashed, banks closed early to prevent a run on accounts, and people lined up at ATMs only to find that the machines were out of cash. Some gas stations charged up to six dollars a gallon, gun shops sold the shelves bare, and grocery stores sold out of water and basic food products as panic-stricken consumers tried to prepare themselves for the unknown. Schools across the nation closed with huge security concerns for the safety of children. Every airport closed, leaving hundreds of thousands of businesspeople and tourists stranded around the country. For the first time in our history, a terrorist organization had assaulted and murdered American citizens on their way to work and school. Chaos and confusion reigned for everyone everywhere.

Finding Comfort in Chaos

The terrorist attacks killed more than three thousand people. In the middle of the chaos, there were some amazing acts of heroism. We learned about strangers helping each other escape alive from burning buildings, including coworkers carrying people in wheelchairs down ninety flights of stairs. We grieved over the 343 firefighters and 23 police officers who gave their lives to save others. We were amazed at military personnel who crawled under the shattered remains of the Pentagon to reach their comrades and help others get to safety. And then we learned of a new kind of hero, the passengers on United Flight 93, who met together to discuss their options, then voted to recapture a flight from terrorists and repeated the Lord's Prayer as passenger Todd Beamer voiced his last words, "We're ready. . . . Let's roll."

In an instant, Americanism was reborn. Young and old were waving flags and boldly proclaiming that they were proud to be Americans. Bin Laden murdered thousands of people, but in so doing he stirred up the passions of hundreds of millions of others. Foreign terrorists shook everything our country believed that morning, and out of the chaos arose a new belief about America.

Healing at Ground Zero

I am a certified crisis intervention stress debriefer. My training and background had prepared me for catastrophic events like school shootings, plane crashes, bank robberies, traffic fatalities, domestic violence, hurricanes, tornadoes, drug overdoses, murders, drownings, and a host of other man-made or natural disasters, but nothing—absolutely nothing—could prepare me for Ground Zero. Our crisis counseling team consisted of Jennifer Cisney, Tim Clinton, Jim Cress, Arch Hart, Ron Hawkins, June Hunt, Beth Moore, Les Parrott, Gary Smalley, and Norm Wright. We went specifically to train over one thousand members of the clergy and helping professions on how to deal with human suffering and tragedy. We talked with first responders from the New York City Fire Department and people who were able to escape with their lives from the World Trade Center. Later I was able to counsel with firefighters and law enforcement and rescue workers down on the "pile," as the main recovery site of the collapsed towers was called. It changed my life. And the healing power of belief will change your life as well.

The hidden power of belief was what motivated firefighters, emergency medical personnel, steel workers, and truckers to pick through the rubble of over two billion pounds of shattered steel, concrete, and glass spread out over sixteen acres. Mayor Rudy Giuliani called it "Ground Zero" because of the unbelievable destruction, which went on for city block after city block of Lower Manhattan. I just couldn't take in all of the images at once, and it was as difficult to hear the stories from the survivors. The "pile" was over nine stories tall and looked like a ghostly scene from the worst horror movie you can imagine. The scene was surrealistic and created intense questions about what to believe in light of such bizarre destruction.

There was honor at Ground Zero. When a body was recovered, the remains were placed in a body bag, then on a stretcher, and then carefully draped with an American flag. The equipment in that area was shut down, and everyone stood at attention and saluted the fallen victim. While other parts of the pile were grinding and moving (we could feel the unstable ground constantly shake and rumble beneath our feet), the body recovery team brought a solemn silence and reverence to the disaster site. It was humbling to stand and salute a victim I didn't know, and it was a powerful reminder that life is very short and uncertain. Watching the body recovery team made us question our deepest beliefs as well as our own mortality. It made us redefine our priorities, which caused us to live differently.

Crisis Reveals What You Believe

Ground Zero revealed what we believed. I remember talking to a young firefighter named Matt who wept as he described how watching the body recovery impacted him. He instinctively reached out to hug me while he wept, while truck drivers and other firefighters just walked by. We were allowed to be real and express our pain on the pile. The terrorists may have meant to destroy America, but it seems they did the opposite, since both young and old are questioning what it means to believe in America and what it means to believe in God. These words from King David brought comfort during those days. Perhaps they will encourage you in your journey today as well: "He does not fear bad news, nor live in dread of what may happen. For he is settled in his mind that Jehovah will take care of him. That is why he is not afraid, but can calmly face his foes" (Ps. 112:7–8 TLB).

I have shared these stories from Ground Zero for two reasons. First, the events of that morning taught all of us that nothing in life is certain. The terrorist attacks made us acutely aware that we need to spend every minute wisely. Reflecting on this tragedy will help each of us to stay motivated toward personal growth and change. Second, the next secret in the success formula is about the power of belief, and nothing in modern times has impacted the thinking of people in the United States as much as the events on and after September 11, 2001. The terrorist attacks made us deal with our beliefs, because we had no choice but to deal with what mattered the most in our lives.

I teach a business seminar entitled "Success Comes in a B.O.X.," in which I share the formula needed to achieve greater success in life. I have presented this seminar to hundreds of people, and now I want to share the key ingredients with you: *belief, opportunity*, and *excellence*. The success formula begins with your belief system, which leads to the next secret on our journey to the life you have always wanted.

 The fifth success secret is that belief is your hidden source of inner strength.

Your core beliefs are the foundation of the important things in your life. Priorities, values, and convictions are established from our early childhood experiences as well as exposure to positive or negative role models. What you believe about education, marriage, hard work, money, reading, travel, politics, and religion, as well as a thousand other subjects, ultimately will be reflected in how you live. When you clearly discover what you believe and then begin to live it out, you will find a hidden source of strength.

You may never have spent any time at all examining your beliefs, much less attempting to live in a manner consistent with those values. This is critically important, because the lack of personal insight is why so many people are unhappy. If you never take time to examine what you believe, you will be like a beach ball on a windy day, bouncing from place to place until something pops you. Perhaps that is what former Beatle John Lennon meant when he said, "Life is what happens to you while you're busy making other plans." I have been to the street corner where he was murdered and seen the bronze marker placed as a tribute to his career. He didn't know that he was walking downstairs to die by an assassin's bullet. That is a lesson in why you must begin now to live your life to the fullest. "Life" happens to the rich, poor, famous, and unknown. What you believe about your life will make it better or worse, which is why I call belief a hidden power.

Belief Brings Blessings

The good news is that you can always be improving and building up your belief system as you build toward your potential. This is important, because your belief will become your greatest strength or your greatest weakness. You can't beat it. Belief will win every time. If you believe that you ultimately will win at an event, you have a hidden source of power in your performance. If you believe you are going to lose, you are dragging an anchor that will limit, if not destroy, your chances of ever becoming successful. Your belief casts a vote either for your success or against it. If you believe that God is with you, then you have an even greater opportunity to experience success in your day-to-day life, because you will be on the lookout for his blessings and will feel a deeper sense of peace in your daily life.

Author Pat Morley reflects on finding a deeper level of his belief in God by pursuing what he calls a moment of humility:

> The moment of humility is an instant of clarity. The heavens briefly open and we see God in a larger way. This moment comes from considering two things—our own mortality and the awesome nature of God—and more so the latter. We contemplate God through prayer, Bible reading, singing, journaling our thoughts, or meditation upon the wonders of creation. We say, "I will not yield to any ordinary day. I will stay with God until by contemplating Him I am

struck with a moment of awe, of transcendence, of being overwhelmed, of sensing a deep gratitude, of a desire to praise and worship."[1]

Your belief in God will bring you comfort during any experience of life. This is illustrated beautifully by a story Robert Ketchum tells about a Sunday school teacher who asked her group of children if anyone could quote the entire Twenty-third Psalm. A golden-haired, four-and-a-half-year-old girl was among those who raised their hands. A bit skeptical, the teacher asked if she could really quote the entire psalm. The little girl came to the front of the room, faced the rest of the class, made a perky little bow, and said, "The Lord is my shepherd; that's all I want." She bowed again and went and sat down. What great insight! If God is our Shepherd through every event of life, who could ask for anything more? Knowing God gives a deeper meaning to life, which always leads to greater success.[2]

General William Booth, founder of the Salvation Army, described the belief that motivated him to reach out to help with the massive needs he saw in the inner city. "While women weep, as they do now, I'll fight. While little children go hungry, as they do now, I'll fight. While men go to prison, in and out, in and out, as they do now, I'll fight. While there is a poor lost girl upon the streets, while there remains one dark soul without the light of God, I'll fight. I'll fight to the very end!" And he did just that. General Booth died in 1912 after dedicating his life to helping those less fortunate than himself. His powerful belief continued beyond his death, and his work still goes on. For more than 125 years, the Salvation Army has helped people fight against the evils of hunger, poverty, disaster, substance abuse, and sin with a message of hope through Christ. Because this one man believed, thousands of people are still being helped through his vision of compassion.

Changing Your Belief about a Cash-Flow Crunch

Believing differently will help you to behave differently. You can instantly reshape your belief about a problem or difficulty with this hidden power. For instance, if you are financially discouraged, considering another perspective will give you the power to change your feelings. Think through the following illustration and then see how you feel.

> If we could shrink the earth's population to a village of precisely 100 people, with all the existing human ratios remaining the same, it would look something like the following:
>
> There would be 60 Asians, 12 Europeans, 15 from the western hemisphere (9 Latin Americans, 5 North Americans, and 1 Oceanian), and 13 Africans.
>
> 50 would be female, 50 would be male.
>
> 80 would be non-white, 20 would be white.
>
> 67 would be non-Christian, 33 would be Christian.
>
> 20 people would earn 89% percent of the entire world's wealth.
>
> 25 would live in substandard housing, 17 would be unable to read, 13 would suffer from malnutrition, 1 would die within the year, 2 would give birth within the year, 2 would have a college education, 4 would own a computer.[3]

No doubt your own financial situation will not seem so bleak when you consider the plight of those much less fortunate. Now how do you feel about the opportunities you enjoy every day? How does it affect your ideas about the words *safe*, *comfortable*, *well-off*, *protected*, and *happy*? Do you see how a slight adjustment in your thinking will lead to radical changes in how you feel and ultimately in how you act? I hope so. You have just taken a crash course in the power of belief and attitude adjustment. Author David Schwartz says, "Where success is concerned, people are not measured in inches or pounds, or college degrees, or family background. They are measured by the size of their thinking. How big we think determines the size of our accomplishments."

The following formula will help you to capture this power regardless of the circumstances you or your team may be facing.

$$B = B$$

Belief = Behavior

This principle will speed you on toward greater success, because it will help you have the energy to move beyond any of the self-destructive patterns we have previously discussed. If you know your beliefs and live them, your behavior will match. You will feel the incredible power of living out what you believe. This correlation of belief and behavior will help you to live more consistently on the journey to the life you want. Abraham Lincoln said it best: "Right makes might." When you and I decide to live exactly like we believe, we have a vast source of hidden power.

The people at Ground Zero discovered that truth. In the midst of a crisis situation, total strangers who had not begun their day with the notion that they should help carry a senior adult down fifty flights of stairs discovered that they in fact had already deeply believed that they should help people they had never met. Firefighters held on to each other in the stairwells as a building crashed to the ground below. What did they believe in those last seconds of life? It showed in their behavior. By charging into a burning skyscraper to help others get out, they showed that deep in their hearts they were men and women of courage. Their behavior revealed their deepest beliefs. It doesn't mean they weren't scared as they held on to each other for support as the buildings swayed and fell. I suspect that they were horrified. But their terror about the critical situation didn't change their belief; it revealed it, and then as they took action, it deepened it.

What about you? If I met you later today and produced a video clip of your behaviors that had been secretly taped the day before, would you look like a success seeker? Would your daily activities resemble those of a winner? Would I see in you the lifestyle of one who is living out his or her dreams, or would I see quite the opposite? Remember that the power of belief works both ways—for good or for evil—which will make your world either a better or worse place.

Here's how the belief formula works.

If you believe it, you live it.

I believe I can make a difference = I work hard.
I believe I should act responsibly = I act responsibly.

I believe reading is a key to lasting success = I read.

I believe in the value of people = I treat others with respect.

I believe I should help others = I help people in need as I can.

I believe I should manage money wisely = I don't waste money.

I believe body care is important = I eat, sleep, and exercise well.

I believe family relationships are important = I spend time with my family.

I believe God is an important part of my life = I worship God regularly.

I believe my opportunities increase as I network = I network in my business.

I believe in saving money for emergencies = I save money and don't touch it.

I believe life is short and should be filled with meaning = I don't waste time.

I believe communication is the key to better relationships = I communicate.

I believe I am a person of great worth = I value my life and manage it wisely.

I believe I am a success = I live like a success.

So how did you do? I suspect that you are beginning to see that it is pretty easy to figure out what you believe, because all you have to do is pay attention and watch how you live, eat, spend, talk, sleep, drive, and work. If you found some inconsistencies, don't panic. You are not alone, because everyone has key issues he or she needs to focus on and then modify to have a better life.

Belief Brings a Longer Life and Lasting Legacy

Changing your belief system may even save your life. Too often we hear stories of nice people who ignored their belief system and pushed their life to the limits only to crash and lose their life. Think of a few people who went beyond the limits of commonly held beliefs about body care and physical health. Take, for example, Jim Henson, the creator of the Muppets, who died from pneumonia. I remember watching his memorial service and hearing different people express how they wished he had slowed down to take care of his health instead of pushing his body beyond the limit and dying so young. His legacy lives on, but how much better it would have been if he had been able to enjoy the success with his friends and family?

I've read similar comments about the driven actor John Belushi, who was begged by his friends to stop abusing cocaine. The drug allowed him to have more energy as well as a superhuman feeling of escaping from his problems. That worked until he died a needless death from abusing drugs for too long and believing he could beat them.

Another tragic example was stock car racer Dale Earnhardt, who pushed himself and his car to the limit as he tried to win the Daytona 500 and then tragically hit the wall and died instantly in front of millions of his fans. One has to wonder how much better off he and his family would have been if he hadn't pushed beyond the laws of speed and gravity on those final laps. Sadly, he had no chance to make another choice to allow him to race again.

Success Starts with What You Believe

The above-mentioned people are very public and tragic examples of pushing your life and body to the limit; but there are millions of others who may be closer to where you live.

- Think of the businessman who regularly works more than sixty hours a week to make money to buy things he never has time to enjoy.
- Think of the woman who works tirelessly to have a "perfect" house but in the process drives her family and friends away because they are too messy. She may have a beautiful house but misses out on having a warm and loving home.
- Think of the millions of Americans who watch too much television, run up debt on their credit cards, and eat the wrong foods while believing that "one day" they will exercise self-discipline and get another chance.

Wrong beliefs lead down the path to a wasted life. That's sad, because a change in belief about what is important in their lives would have led to different priorities and decisions. Making lifestyle changes would have led to more success.

When you see the power of connecting beliefs to behavior, you will see the development of greater success in your life. Furthermore, when you become clear on what you believe, you can help others deal with their beliefs. If you are trying to help a family member, or a member of your corporate team, or perhaps a niece or nephew, or your marriage partner, it will be easier if you know what you believe. Jesus Christ said, "If a blind man leads a blind man, both will fall into a pit"

(Matt. 15:14). When you begin to push yourself in the area of expressing your personal beliefs, you will go to a new level of success, and you will likely take your closest companions with you on the journey. Viktor Frankl expressed this when he said, "If you treat people to a vision of themselves, if you apparently overrate them, you make them become what they are capable of becoming. If you take them as they should be, you help them become what they can be."

Three-Part Coaching Strategy

Here's a coaching strategy I use to evaluate if you are experiencing the hidden power of a personal belief system.

First is *direct awareness*. Open your mind to the possibility that your belief about a situation has the power to change how effectively you deal with that situation. Use this phrase: "Consider the possibility of. . . ." Becoming aware that a better life is possible for you will stretch your thinking to a new level.

Second is *honest assessment*. Be candidly tuned in to what you believe. This is an important step, because many people have never sat down with a legal pad and listed their personal beliefs. Focus on what you believe about every significant part of your life by listing short statements beginning with "I believe. . . ." What you believe has great power, so don't skip this important stage of researching your core beliefs. It will change you and take your thinking—and living—to a new level.

Third is *aggressive action*. Once you establish what you believe, take immediate action. Don't let another day slip by without focusing on what you can do to improve your situation in life and to add value to others. Use positive words and powerful verbs that show movement toward a better place. For example, "I eat healthy every time;" "I love my friends and connect with them regularly;" "I spend my money wisely;" "I love God and live out his principles;" "I enjoy every day of the life I have been given." When you know what to do, get up and do it. Action will race you toward your goals, and you will begin to see dramatic results in your life. The results will encourage you to stay with the power of belief, and you will continue to live a new way with a new level of success.

The General George S. Patton Museum at Fort Knox, Kentucky, contains the historical record of this controversial man and his ability to aggressively take action. The walls and exhibits reveal the driven nature of this World War II general. His 3rd Army once advanced so far ahead of his supply lines that provisions had to be airlifted to reach them. The 3rd Army gained more ground and took more prisoners than any army in history. Patton was ambitious and was known for using the phrase "Attack, always attack!" during battle. That is the mentality of those who have tapped into the hidden power of belief. They push forward and break all barriers. They literally become unstoppable as they experience the strength of pressing forward toward the successful life they believe in. When you follow the formula of direct awareness, honest assessment, and aggressive action, you will be well on the way to living out the power of your belief system. You will also be on your way to a better life, since you will be benefiting from the hidden power of personal belief.

Consider the success from mapping out a personal belief system reflected in this poem by an unknown author:

A wise man knows how unreliable his wisdom is.

A wise man knows that pride can lead to either honor or shame.

A wise man steers his ambition as if it were a dozer through a schoolyard.

A wise man is conscious that each moment is a passing gift from God.

A wise man is ready to stand alone yet acts in counsel.

A wise man is angered by injustice or evil but submits his anger to the rule of law.

A wise man trusts a wounded bear more than his appetites.

A wise man values character above success.

A wise man will guard his mind as if it were his daughter.

A wise man knows how fickle fame is, how vain is notoriety.

A wise man labors and builds knowing that it will return to dust.

A wise man is ever conscious of the presence of God.

A wise man will pray as a first resort.

A wise man loves one woman as if it were his sole appointment for eternity.

A wise man will father children and then train them as if they were God's.

A wise man will alleviate the suffering of others but never mention his own.

A wise man will utilize his past mistakes as sign-
posts for the future.
A wise man will love and live each day as if it were
his last.

The Pearls have modeled the importance of getting a legal pad out to list personal beliefs. As you list what you believe, you can then begin to map out how those core beliefs will impact your behavior. The *B* in the B.O.X. formula will give you the hidden power to live like a person filled to overflowing with success. Be encouraged at this point in our journey together, because when you master this first step of the success formula, you are well on your way to the next important step—discovering your "opportunity magnet." Are you ready to move on? Do you believe success is really possible?

Good! Then let's keep climbing toward your dreams!

TEN

Secret #6

OPPORTUNITY—
DISCOVERING YOUR
SUCCESS MAGNET

Some of us tend to think, I could have been a success, but I never had the opportunity. I wasn't born into the right family, or I didn't have the money to go to the best school. But when we measure success by the extent we're using what we received, it eliminates frustration.

—Fred Smith

Charles Darrow lost his job in 1931 at the beginning of the worst economic depression in U.S. history. He was broke financially but not broke in his creative ability to see beyond the circumstances to a greater level of success. As the financial pressure increased, so did his creativity. Losing his job eventually made him a multimillionaire.

Unemployment Led to Unusual Wealth

Being laid off led to Darrow's success. He had time—time to sit, time to think, time to create. He sat at his kitchen table and sketched on the oilcloth table covering. He didn't engage in the meaningless doodling of the depressed; rather, he spent hours pretending to be a real estate tycoon, complete with top hat and tails, in fashionable Atlantic City. He was more than just the venture capitalist of the kitchen. He was a designer, dream builder, and yes, game maker. You guessed it—he invented the board game Monopoly while sitting at that table. The real estate properties, houses, hotels, railroads, and even "going to jail" were dreamed up at that table. He didn't stay there for too long, however. His entrepreneurial spirit soared, and he packaged up his idea and took it to corporate America.

Darrow enthusiastically pitched his idea to game giant Parker Brothers, who promptly rejected it! Remember, this was the Great Depression. Unemployment was the worst it had ever been in the United States. Many people didn't have money for food, much less board games. Corporate America said no. So Darrow left and did what any success seeker would do. He took his idea to the streets by building and marketing the game himself. He was successful in spite of the economy, in spite of the rejection of a corporate sponsor, and in spite of the financial pressure that always comes with new projects that are usually short on capital but long on passion.

Darrow's determination paid off. Parker Brothers noticed how successful Darrow was at convincing Americans to escape the financial hardships of the world around them by diving into their own "Monopoly." People loved the game! They could buy, sell, build wealth, or destroy the fortunes of their friends with the roll of a dice. Parker Brothers bought the game in 1935, and the royalties made Darrow a millionaire. The roadblock of losing his job helped him go down a new road to create a game that would become part of Americana. Every time I play the game, I remember that an unemployed success seeker found an opportunity in the middle of a crisis.

Successful people have discovered how to find opportunity regardless of the circumstances. No matter what is going on around them, they know how to pinpoint and then "lock in" on the activities that will lead them to accomplish their goals. This is the next element of the B.O.X. formula, which is also the next secret of success.

The sixth success secret is opportunity.

Successful people know about opportunity. They know how to find it and, more important, what to do with it. Listen to some great thinkers commenting on the power of this secret of success.

To succeed, jump as quickly at opportunities as you do at conclusions.

—Benjamin Franklin

The secret of success is to be ready when your opportunity comes.

—Benjamin Disraeli

Problems are opportunities in work clothes.

—Henry J. Kaiser

There comes a special moment in everyone's life, a moment for which that person was born. That special opportunity, when he seizes it, will fulfill his mission, a mission for which he is uniquely qualified. In that moment, he finds greatness. It is his finest hour.

—Winston Churchill

Become a Creative Visionary

A success seeker always knows how to find opportunity. I challenge you to attempt to think differently about situations, to look for creative opportunities that open new doors to success. This will stretch your thinking, like author Dan Reiland says: "Creative people are different, adventurous, and comfortable with change." To achieve greater success, you will need to think creatively like Walt Disney and become an "imagineer" with your own life. Stretch your thinking by being innovative in finding immediate solutions to complex problems. Read the following problem from an employment exam and see if you can envision a successful way to solve a difficult situation.

You are driving your car on a wild and stormy night. You pass by a bus station and see three people waiting for the bus—an old lady who looks quite ill, as if she is about to die, a doctor who had once saved your life, and a business leader you have been desperately trying to meet. You can only take one passenger in your car. Which one will you choose? (Be prepared to explain your answer.)

Think about it before you continue reading.

Obviously this is a personality test. Think logically through your options. You could pick up the old lady. She is going to die, and ethically you should save her first. You could take the doctor, because he once saved your life. This would be the perfect chance to reward him with a display of your gratitude. However, you could always pay back the doctor in the future, but you may never be able to find a chance to network with the business leader, who may take your company to a new level of financial success, if you pass up this one chance.

As the story goes, the candidate who was eventually hired out of hundreds of applicants did not have to explain his answer. What did he say? He simply answered: "Give the car keys to the doctor. Let him take the old lady to the hospital. I will stay and wait for the bus with the business leader to discuss how we might partner together. The chance to help the old lady by assisting the doctor to save her life would show my character to the business leader and might open even more opportunities to discuss the power of teamwork."

How did you do? Did you think creatively to solve the problem? Did you give up your old limited way of thinking to find a successful solution for everyone in the story? Did you maximize your opportunities to further strengthen your relationships and experience long-term success? Or did you kill off the old lady to pursue your cash-flow goals while rudely ignoring the kindness of the doctor? Did you think in a bigger way that allowed everyone, including you, to win? If so, good, you are beginning to think like a successful visionary. If not, don't give up. Start now to learn from every event and experience happening around you. Become an observer of what works, of what brings results, as well as what doesn't. Success seekers turn their observations into opportunities.

Difficulties Lead to Decisions

Norman Vincent Peale was one of those success seekers. He described himself as a very shy and self-doubting boy who was driven to discover the roots of his low self-esteem. It was through the process of trying to understand and overcome his feelings of timidity that he developed the philosophy of the book *The Power of Positive Thinking*. Peale described it this way: "If a person lives by sensible principles he won't be free from trouble, but he'd know how to handle trouble." The book begins with a single powerful phrase: "Believe in yourself!" First published in 1952, there are now over fifteen million copies in print. This Methodist preacher was one of the first religious leaders in the country to use mass media along with the pulpit to proclaim a message of hope to hurting people. He was able to turn his insecurities into a life lesson to help millions.

Peale's difficulties led him to make the decision to find greater opportunities. You can do the same. Albert Einstein said, "In the middle of difficulty lies opportunity." You can let the challenges of life bring out your best and creatively find even more opportunities for success, or you can curl up in bed and pull the covers over your head.

Finding Your Success Magnet

You can search for opportunities, or you can run from them; sometimes they will even find you. Learning the power of this secret of success will help you every day, because you will be utilizing what I call a "success magnet." Magnets are an unusual force. You can't see magnetic fields, but you know they are always there. A compass, a delicate instrument that automatically points to true north, will expose them. Just as you can always find your way with a compass, you can always find success with your opportunity magnet.

Magnets are very useful. Holistic practitioners use tiny magnets to provide relief from pain in the joints of the body. Mechanics use magnets to retrieve lost parts or tools. Wrecking yards use huge magnets to move junk cars around. The bigger the magnet, the bigger the things you can pick up. Likewise, the bigger your opportunity magnet, the more you will attract the right people and situations to help you toward your destination. One successful thing always leads to another. Just like the magnetic force fields that surround the earth, success always brings more success. It's a law of the universe.

If this process seems radical to you, then consider how one of the most successful and innovative entrepreneurs in the world manages his opportunities. Richard Branson, founder of Virgin Atlantic Airlines, said he learned every day by trying new and different ways of doing things. If someone came to him with a good idea, he didn't send them to more meetings to present it to more groups—he let them get started! That flexibility helped him keep many good employees as well as learn many new ways of succeeding.

One has to admire Branson's enthusiasm! His opportunity magnet kept drawing more and more chances for his business to expand. You too will find that opportunities are everywhere! As you travel along your journey to greater success, you will experience times when everything comes together in a powerful way and the results are magical.

Magical Opportunities Still Happen

In a Florida city not long ago, the Apopka Little League, on a fluke, worked their way up to the Little League World Series. A team of "no-name" twelve-year-olds just kept on winning, beating impossible odds, and shattering statistics. Everything was working for them in spite of incredible obstacles. They were a smaller, less-experienced team who had played together for a shorter time than many of the competitive teams that typically dominate the championship. Their uniforms weren't as nice, and they just didn't fit the image of what you would expect for the "best of the best" in the nation for their sport. That's what made their success so magical!

The excitement was overwhelming as the Apopka community watched these players out-hit, out-field, and generally out-perform their highly favored opponents. It was a Cinderella season! I get chills thinking about the powerful example of this team of twelve-year-olds who went out with a single mission—to win! They played with more heart than any team they faced, and it showed on the scoreboard. Win, win, win! Nothing could stop them. Nothing! They were completely dedicated in their quest to become national champions.

How did they do it? They played as one—one heart, one vision, one focus, one goal! Personal agendas for becoming the "star" of the team were set aside, and this group of dedicated kids showed the world what teamwork was about. These boys became the best of what still makes America the greatest land of opportunity in the world. On any given day on any given ball field in any city, you can find greatness. The greatness of shared vision builds powerful opportunities for the entire team. Everyone wins!

I am happy to have been able to cheer for a team of young people who showed more character and dedication than many pro sports teams. It seems that some teams have a couple of players who sacrifice team goals for their personal dreams at the expense of their teammates, coaches, and owners. Furthermore, the community's economy may be hurt, since losing games results in fewer spectators, which leads to decreased revenues to fuel the jobs associated with that team. And how greedy it is for some players to drive to the games in a luxury vehicle that may cost more than the home of the guy cleaning the ball field rest rooms? When individual players are out "winning" a big name for themselves at the expense of the rest of the organization, that's not success. It's selfishness. Such superficial "success" doesn't last. It can't last, because it violates what successful teams are all about—one another. When individual players try to steal the team's opportunity and turn it into a personal opportunity, they set

---

Say it out loud: "They won together!"

Doesn't it feel good to say that? Wouldn't it be wonderful to say that your family won together? That your company won together? That your marriage won because you and your mate won together? That your community project won because everyone came together? Are you playing on a team with a single purpose? Will your team win together?

---

themselves up for major problems. When you try to cheat the laws of success, the magnet backfires and brings only failure to you.

That is not the story of the 2001 Apopka Little League All-Stars! They and their parents, grandparents, coaches, teachers, and friends will be talking about their win for the rest of their lives. They faced impossible odds and won. They lived the words of the Ashanti proverb "You must act as if it is impossible to fail." They defied the doomsayers who said it couldn't be done. They proved that there is more power in a team of committed twelve-year-olds than bigger, stronger, and faster opponents could ever match. And the best part is that they won together!

Opportunities Reveal the Invisible

"Vision is the art of seeing things invisible." These words from Jonathan Swift reveal how opportunities give a person insight into the obvious things others miss. When you begin to view life as a series of wonderful opportunities, you will see things that absolutely amaze you! I saw this demonstrated recently while flying back from Nashville. An excited five-year-old named Colton was sitting in row 8, seat C. I discovered that he was on his very first flight and was jazzed about everything he saw. His mom told me that Colton had a good imagination as she sort of apologized for his robust enthusiasm. His play-by-play descriptions didn't bother me at all. I enjoyed hearing how in a creative new way he vividly explained things I had seen hundreds of times. He stayed pressed against the window most of the trip and in a Tennessee accent kept saying, "I can see the whole world from up here. It's cool!"

You know, Colton was right on target. If you really open your eyes, you can see the whole world. You can see opportunities and possibilities you never knew existed! When you see the big picture, you aren't as worried about the roadblocks. You stay focused on finding success where you are today and then getting ready for more success tomorrow. Difficulties in life could steal your focus, but I challenge you to not let that happen. To protect your opportunity magnet from losing energy for finding positive answers, use this strategy.

$\rightarrow$ Potential Level

$\rightarrow$ Problem Level

Stay above the problem level of life by viewing the potential level. As you get above the problems, you will see the unique opportunities and options for solving those problems. That's how email, microwave popcorn, cordless telephones, remote controls, handheld computers, and portable global positioning systems were invented. Poet William Blake said, "What is now proved was once only imagined." Thousands of products and services are created when success seekers use their creativity to imagine solutions to problem situations. These people move beyond panic by grabbing a legal pad and mapping out powerful strategies. They know that gigantic challenges create even greater opportunities for those who have mastered this secret of success. As you begin to use the *O* in the B.O.X. formula to see the invisible, you will begin to do the impossible. You will discover more fun than you ever imagined, because every day will bring you more joy. You will spend your energy looking for possibilities in your circumstances instead of whining about the pain and pressure. You will begin to see your blessings instead of fussing and complaining about the commonplace problems everyone has to deal with, and you will be on your way to a better life.

Luck or Labor?

Oprah Winfrey is a phenomenon. Having overcome the difficulties of childhood abuse to move into the highly competitive world of television, she continues to shatter records in broadcast journalism and publishing. How could an overweight and unknown woman take on the number one talkshow host in the country? You may remember that when Oprah began broadcasting in Chicago, her cross-town rival was Phil Donahue. She had no way of attracting influential and powerful guests like her competition could, so she found another opportunity: She told the stories of people who had overcome difficulties. She cried along with them and told her own stories of moving beyond pain to find peace and in the process touched lives and made a difference. She invested in other people by adding value with her programs and resources. Was it luck for her or just hard labor? Her answer: "Luck is when preparation meets opportunity." Every time I watch her program or read her magazine, I take away some creative ideas about moving beyond difficulties to find greater success, because she is a success seeker who shares her insights with others.

If you are going to enjoy greater success, you will have to let go of the notion that luck has everything to do with accomplishment, that you will be standing in the right place at the right time and money will fall out of the sky with your name on it. This commonly held view is why people spend millions of dollars on lotteries. Don't forget that the money they "give away" comes from people purchasing the tickets. It's called gaming because it involves a roll of the dice. Read the fine print, and it will plainly say that you may not win. Yet many people would rather spend their time and energy trying to find "luck" instead of doing the work to discover opportunity.

If you just stand around and hope and pray that you will be successful, you are ignoring something I figured out at the bank one day. I patiently stood at a teller window for a few minutes until my banker told me that line was closed. I felt embarrassed for a minute but learned a good lesson. Simply put, the longer you wait in line, the greater the likelihood that you are standing in the wrong line. Opportunity is like that. If you stand around and wait for it, it won't show up, but failure might. My friend Pat Williams, the NBA visionary who helped create the Orlando Magic, has some practical advice about waiting for luck to mystically bring people to the events RDV Sports presents: "If you don't market, a terrible thing happens. Nothing." He has that slogan on a desk sign to remind him every day to tell the story of the Magic and the WNBA Miracle.

The desire to push beyond crossing your fingers and feeling lucky to aggressively and boldly claiming the victory is essential for success in sports or life. I saw this theme on a billboard the other day for the National Arena Football Champion Orlando Predators: "Be a Predator or Be Prey!" Race toward your desires of success or get run over by those who will claim the prize.

Details Determine Destiny

I have the motto "Details determine destiny" on my desk, because I know that a focused leader follows up on opportunities that come along. This will not be easy, because there are many possibilities but only time enough to effectively develop a few. Sometimes painful events come that seem to interrupt your plans for success. Visionaries know how to manage the discomfort of discouragement and keep pressing forward to other possibilities. Tracking each detail and every lead will prepare you in case things don't work out the way you anticipated. Television sports anchor Pat Clark knows this secret. He was leaving work to emcee a charity fundraiser when he received the news that he was being fired from his job. The great risk of television journalism is that your career stability hinges on ratings instead of personality. Although he knew he would be unemployed on Monday, at the close of the charity event, he read with great passion the following poem by Veronica A. Shoffstall:

> After a while, you learn the subtle difference between holding a hand and chaining a soul.
> You begin to learn that kisses aren't contracts and presents aren't promises.

> Learn to accept your defeats with your head up
>> and your eyes open—with the grace of an
>> adult, not the grief of a child.
> You build your roads on today, because tomor-
>> row's roads are too uncertain for plans.
> So plant your own garden and decorate your own
>> soul instead of waiting for someone to bring
>> you flowers.
> And learn you really can endure, that you really
>> are strong and you really do have worth.

Clark used disappointment as a stepping-stone to suc-cess instead of crying over his high-profile job coming to an end. He searched for opportunities and networked to find another position. He eventually bounced back and went to another sportscasting job. Everyone admires public people who show leadership and personal growth through the dif-ficult seasons of their life. Conversely, most people disrespect celebrities who don't learn character and life lessons when they fall from grace.

Squeezing Every Ounce of Opportunity

Because you don't get a second chance at life, it is imperative to squeeze every drop of opportunity out of situations. My friend John Murphy says that learning to squeeze the most out of life means that you won't skip "meaning-full" activities like playing with or reading to your children because you are busy with "meaning-less" things like watching one more sporting event or sitcom. Successful people have learned how to fill up their lives with meaning-fullness. For instance, they might call a friend just to say hello instead of sitting down and feeling lonely, bored, or unhappy with their lives. When you can balance your daily activities by putting them in two categories—things with and without meaning—you will have the time of your life!

Personal meditation is one of the greatest sources of guidance for protecting against meaningless activity. A personal quiet time of reading and reflection each day will keep your ambition and drive "centered" on your life values and personal mission. This routine will keep you going strong as you tap into a source of spiritual strength, one of the energy sources of success seekers. Try a quiet time of prayer and meditation today and see how much more peaceful and focused you feel all day long.

Remember that lasting success has a strong commitment to relationships and balanced time with others. This view of success will help you to not win the prize only to celebrate alone. It will protect you when you are tempted to give up on sleep, exercise, and personal meditation to accomplish some goal at the expense of burning out and ending up exhausted in a hospital. It doesn't matter if you had the most profitable statistics in the history of your company if you end up in the ER with a tube stuck up your nose to keep you alive. If you are dying from overwork, you are not successful. The great educator Booker T. Washington said, "Never let work drive you; master it and keep it in complete control."

Your Life Clock Is Ticking

Why the urgency to manage events and emotions to live your life well? One reason: The clock is ticking for you. The following illustration implies the importance of managing every moment as you move toward a destination of greater success.

If life is a clock and you are born at 12:00 A.M. and die at midnight, you have 24 hours. If the average life span is 72 years, each hour represents 3 years. For instance, if you are 39, it is 1 P.M.; if you are 51, it is 5 P.M.; and if you are 60, it's already 8:00 P.M. If you measure life like a clock, it passes rather quickly. So where are you on the "clock" of life?

Discovering and managing opportunity take insight, skill, patience, and a clear vision to see things the way they can be. When you learn to see the possibilities instead of just racing on to the next event in your busy life, you will open up a whole new world.

Are you ready for the final secret?

Then open your eyes wide to the possibility of a better life!

ELEVEN

Secret #7

EXCELLENCE—
LIVING THE LIFE
YOU'VE ALWAYS WANTED

The quality of a person's life is in direct proportion to their commitment to excellence, regardless of their chosen field of endeavor.

—Vince Lombardi

Swimmers use remarkable self-discipline to keep pushing their bodies even though they can't see an immediate reward for their effort. They have to ignore others to focus on pushing themselves to the edge of their performance envelope. Swimmers train like machines; every stroke, every kick, every breath has to be carefully measured to achieve maximum performance. They also must push beyond the discomfort of very cold water to glide through a pool every day for months in preparation for a few minutes of competition. If you have ever wondered why a water sport competition is called a "heat," just attend a swim meet. You will quickly discover that champion swimmers come to "burn up" the water. I have been a pool marshal for the Florida High School Athletic Association and have seen that these athletes don't come to the state competition to swim—they come to win.

Swimming is a mental sport as much as a physical one. The swimmers show their strong desire to win before they ever get in the water. They wear outrageous slogans on their T-shirts to "psych-out" their opponents:

- The meek may inherit the earth, but they will never rule the water.
- Warning: The surgeon general said nothing about smoking your opponent.
- I live on a tough street and the further you go down it the tougher it gets. I live on the last house on that street!

These slogans were designed to intimidate, but the message on the T-shirt of the state champions was consistently the same: "Winners Train Every Day." The best of the best in any sport are the ones who have the self-discipline and drive to train aggressively. They prepare hundreds of hours before competing, and they win. One of those swimmers broke a national record twice in the same day! Miami's Christina

Swindle broke the national record for the girls' 50-yard free-style in the preliminary then came back in the championship to shatter her own record. People were shouting, cheering, and mobbing her. Camera flashes were illuminating the pool like a fireworks display when her mother broke through the crowd to hug her. Champions push themselves to train hard because they are competing against their own potential and playing to win—every time.

Success Icebergs

The dictionary is the only place where success comes before work. The effort to achieve excellence is part of the joy of living a life of meaning and fulfillment. Success doesn't arrive when you are handed the trophy. Success is when you get up early and take the right steps to live like a winner. The trophy time is the end of an event or project signifying that it is time to go back to practice to find success for the next event.

Learn to view success as an iceberg. The tip shows at all times and represents a fraction of what is underneath. A giant iceberg that stands twenty stories above the water has hundreds of feet of solid ice underneath holding up the tip for all to see. You are like that iceberg. As you discipline yourself to live a life of hard work that is focused on your destination of success, you will do hundreds of things no one will ever see. An insightful person knows that true success is bigger than most people realize and that it requires a daily discipline to move forward to achieve goals.

Successful people live differently because they believe that achievement comes in proportion to their commitment to hard work and personal excellence. Oliver Wendell Holmes said, "It is effort that makes the inevitable come to pass." Successful people achieve results because of their extraordinary effort.

When you are living a successful life, then get ready for more excitement, enthusiasm, exhilaration, and energy! Are you ready to pick up the remaining key to unlock a better life? Then get ready for the final secret of success.

 ## The seventh success secret is excellence.

The B.O.X. formula works only when you apply the X—excellence. Become a person known for achievement, and you will find that success begins to show up more and more often. This is true in business, family relationships, and personal health. Push yourself to achieve your best, not just sometimes, but every time! Personal excellence will enhance professional performance. As you implement a commitment to quality in everything you do, from practicing behind the scenes to performing on the platform, you will notice two things. First, your successes will come much more often and usually be greater than you imagined. Second, you will notice how poorly others follow this success strategy.

Some people play the game of life to win, and others play with just enough effort not to lose. That's not successful, that's slothful. Lazy people frequently attempt to get by with sloppy work. In fact, they spend their time and creativity thinking of ways to avoid being a self-disciplined person of excellence. If they worked as hard at their goals as they do in trying to avoid hard work, they would be among the rising superstars in their industry. Remember, if you skip work, success will skip you. Here are some of the craziest excuses I've heard for why people don't come to work.

- I can't come in to work today because I'll be stalking my previous boss, who fired me for not showing up for work. Okay?
- I'm stuck in the blood pressure machine down at Walgreens.
- The dog ate my car keys. We're going to hitchhike to the vet.
- Constipation has made me a walking time bomb.

While these excuses make you laugh, thousands of people have tried to avoid work by using similar lame excuses. They may not have realized it, but their irresponsible behavior meant that they would forfeit a successful life. There is nothing funny about failure, and no one laughs about missing out on the enjoyment of a better life.

No Excellence	=	Poor Practice
Poor Practice	=	Poor Performance
Poor Performance	=	No Success

The bottom line is that practice not only makes perfect, it also makes success come more often. Advertising guru David Ogilvy knows this, because his client list is a "who's who" of successful corporations, including Rolls Royce. He says of excellence in advertising:

You don't stand a tinker's chance of producing successful advertising unless you start by doing your homework. I have always found this extremely tedious, but there is no substitute for it. First, study the product you are going to advertise. The more you know about it, the more likely you are to come up with a big idea for selling it. . . . If you are too lazy to do this kind of homework, you may occasionally *luck* into a successful campaign, but you will run the risk of skidding about on what my brother Francis called "the slippery surface of irrelevant brilliance."[1]

Passion Is Evidenced by Practice

The commitment to personal excellence is a way of life that doesn't require luck because it's all about work—continual research, focus groups, beta testing, benchmarking, practical application, testing, retesting, and learning from every failed attempt. Striving for excellence is tough sometimes, but working to reach the goal is part of the satisfaction. I have seen this vividly in a daily routine modeled by my nephew Christopher. He is a great pianist who has received spontaneous standing ovations while playing before groups of three hundred to three thousand. He is only seventeen years old, yet he makes the piano come alive with excitement in a style very similar to that of John Tesh. It is a joy to hear him play, not only because I am proud of his accomplishment, but also because I know that he practices the piano for hours every day. It is his passion, which is evidenced by his practice. If you want to see if someone is truly successful, pay attention to how much that person practices, researches, studies, prepares, explores, strategizes, and implements. If this sounds like a full day's work, you are right! Success requires a complete commitment to excellence.

I had a chance to ask the 1970s singing sensation Donny Osmond about his amazing ability to bounce back in the difficult entertainment industry of music and television. I asked him to describe how he had attained such success and longevity. He rather humbly said, "If this business was easy, everybody would still be in it. You gotta keep trying." Few performers have tried, failed, and tried again like Donny. Yet that is the reason we know his name out of the thousands of pop stars who have come and gone since Donny and Marie were singing about being "a little bit country and a little bit rock and roll" years ago. In spite of numerous setbacks, financial difficulties, and personal problems, his commitment to excellence has kept him energized to press on. His passion is evidenced by how hard he continues to work on his long-term goals.

Manageable and Expected Roadblocks

You likely agree with the importance of using the B.O.X. formula to discover more success yet are trying to figure out how to become excellent every time at everything. Stop focusing on perfection or controlling life events. The X is about you becoming your personal best. Sometimes that can't happen because of the roadblocks that stand in your way. Some are big, others aren't. Some of the difficulties in life are to be expected, like being misunderstood, having difficulty finding a good career "fit," experiencing poor communication between you and your loved ones, struggling with genetic predispositions to diabetes, heart disease, or obesity, or being weighed down by limitations of time and money. Other roadblocks are sudden and a lot harder to avoid, such as corporate downsizing, broken relationships, car accidents, miscarriages, IRS audits, and stress-related illnesses like chronic fatigue, ulcers, or panic disorder. Then there are huge roadblocks like cancer, bankruptcy, or divorce, any of which can occur suddenly even though you were working to prevent it. You will have roadblocks, but you must get past them. It is a necessary part of becoming a success seeker.

Have you ever faced roadblocks that were so big that just looking at them seemed to steal your energy to move forward? Have you felt so overwhelmed with pressure and problems that you didn't even know where to start? Maybe you thought you could handle it and then realized too late that you were in the deep end of the pool swimming with the sharks. How can you achieve excellence when there are so many roadblocks to success? Author Phyllis Bottome gives the answer: "There are two ways of meeting difficulties; alter the difficulties or alter the way you meet them."

Roadblocks prevent success from happening by pushing excellence to the side as a nonessential. When the goal is survival, personal performance suffers. So what can you do to move beyond the roadblocks? First, know that we all have them and that they come from many places. Here is an exercise to help you identify possible roadblocks to your creative ability to uncover and discover success in spite of any circumstance. Check any indicator that would influence your thinking, especially if you consider it to be a weakness that limits your effectiveness or personal excellence. These are your manageable roadblocks.

Possible Success Roadblocks

___ belief system (negative attitude)

___ physical health (illness, disease, or pain)

___ self-talk (I'm a loser, unlucky, ugly, etc.)

___ past mistakes or poor choices (didn't finish college, was arrested, quit jobs)

___ current life stressors (debts, coparenting, disorganized, chronic worry)

___ past failures (rejected, fired, bankrupt, foreclosed upon)

___ stuffed emotions (anger, bitterness, resentment, jealousy)

___ spiritual emptiness ("Even if he exists, I know that God doesn't like me.")

___ compulsive behaviors ("I just have to smoke; it's how I deal with my life.")

___ actions of others ("He did this to me, and it ruined my life.")

___ fear of confronting ("I just wish I could give her a piece of my mind!")

___ secrets ("If anyone ever found out about this, I'd be ruined.")

___ fears and doubts ("I could never be good at that—no way.")

___ feeling powerless to change ("It's over for me; I'll never measure up!")

How many roadblocks did you identify? Whether it was a few or every single one, you now recognize some things that have held you back from living the life you've always desired. I called these manageable roadblocks because you can identify and target which ones need to be moved. You can begin to tackle the things that have held you back with a direct plan of action. A key to what makes the "great ones" great is their ability to work toward success in spite of their circumstances. Whatever comes, successful people have learned to plan ways to deal with the problem and then get to work on it—no excuses, just excellence.

Success seekers have an "attitude of gratitude" during difficult times while aggressively working to get past the roadblocks. Having a failure on your path to a more success-ful life is common. Everyone has roadblocks. For example, seminar and training guru Fred Pryor watched the company he founded go through bankruptcy and then led it back to becoming an industry leader. Jay Leno couldn't pass an em-ployment test for Woolworth's. Barbara Walters was once told to "stay out of television," and Jerry Seinfeld once sold lightbulbs to make a living. Paul Newman was kicked off his high school football team, so he started acting just to pass the time. Teddy Roosevelt shared this thought about failure and success: "It is hard to fail, but it is worse never to have tried to succeed. In this life we get nothing, save by effort."

Everyone hits roadblocks, and sometimes they get knocked down. When successful people get knocked down, they get back up. The roadblock of failure can be a powerful teacher if you learn to refocus and prepare for the next opportunity.

Unmanageable and Unexpected Roadblocks

Now that you have identified some expected roadblocks to work on, let's move on to the unexpected ones. They come in two sizes—small and gigantic. Actively manage the small ones that are easier to move out of your path—things like not making it to the dry cleaners before they close, being stuck in traffic, or paying a bill late. While these may sound like little irritations, they can become a roadblock. Not making it to the dry cleaners on time could mean that you don't have your "power suit" to wear to an important meeting where you must look your best. Being stuck in traffic could make you late for a job interview, and you could miss out on a great career opportunity. Paying a bill late, which is reflected on your overall credit, could create doubt from a lender and cost you thousands of dollars if you are trying to get a line of credit to start a new business. Little roadblocks can become big ones that could block you from reaching your goals.

Major roadblocks can stop you cold. Most of these are unexpected problems that tend to change your life forever, but when you are learning to find success in any circumstance, you can make a positive change. Consider the story of John Muir, who became America's greatest conservationist because of a roadblock from an injury. He was born in Scotland and immigrated with his parents to a farm in Wisconsin when he was eleven years old. He was mostly self-educated, rather eccentric, and didn't always fit in with the crowd. Muir seriously injured one of his eyes while working in a wagon parts factory in Indianapolis and had to leave work for many months to heal. His injury gave him time to take long nature walks, and he eventually traveled to the Sierra Nevada Mountains in California to find physical and spiritual rest. He found his purpose for living in those mountains and became the greatest environmentalist of his era and one of the strongest voices for protecting the environment of all time.

In 1901 Muir compelled President Roosevelt to travel with him to Yosemite to camp out under the stars to examine the dangers to the area from lumbering and sheep grazing. Roosevelt was so moved that he joined Muir in his fight to have Congress set aside national parks for the benefit of future generations. If you have ever enjoyed visiting any one of our nation's beautiful national parks, you can thank John Muir, a man who didn't give up on life because of an injury.

His roadblock turned him in a new direction where he found his life's passion. Although not rich in finances, he helped a young American nation find a balance between development and conservation and was wealthy in the lasting influence he left to millions. Of his career-ending injury and decision to move west, Muir said, "I might have become a millionaire, but I decided to become a tramp."

Warning: Resentment Steals Success

Like John Muir, you may have had an injury that hindered your ability to work. You may have lost a job over it and are still angry about your financial losses. You may be in the heat of litigation right now thinking of how you will get satisfaction for the pain you've endured. You may rub your hands in glee just thinking about how your former employer is going to suffer, like you have suffered, when the multimillion-dollar judgment is declared. I challenge you to give up on being a bitter, hate-filled person. Don't go another day carrying your hurt and hatred, because you can't carry hatred and happiness at the same time. You can only carry one emotion, so if your heart is full of resentment, there is no room for rejoicing.

A better perspective is that of the Reverend John Bradford, who lived in England from 1510 to 1555, a time when injustice ruled and people held little regard for life. It is said that on seeing evildoers taken to the place of execution, he would exclaim, "But for the grace of God there goes John Bradford." Bradford had a humble spirit, which helped him move beyond roadblocks by reflecting a deeper understanding of pain and perversity in humans. Learn that the world doesn't revolve around the happiness of any one person and that bad things happen to all people. The world contains billions of human beings who must make choices every day about how they will face the obstacles in their paths. Each person on this planet has a story, and as we learned earlier, those stories have power. Bradford's story still challenges individuals to examine their own lives before sitting in judgment on others.

If someone has wronged you, it is right to attempt to resolve the situation, but don't spend your life fighting to prove that someone else is to blame for your problems. People of excellence are more likely to cut their losses than they are to stop and curse. Your success is too important to sacrifice time and energy in petty arguments. I am not saying that those who do wrong should not be held accountable for irresponsible behavior. When wrong is done, the courts are open for judges and juries to sort through the details. Rather, I am coaching you to let go of a wagonload of hatred and resentment. Being bitter doesn't hurt the other person; it hurts you! Medical researchers believe that your chances for serious disease may increase when you are full of hate. Letting go of the roadblock of resentment will likely improve your physical as well as emotional health. You will feel better if you learn to let go of your painful past failures. If you don't let go of those disappointments, you will find it impossible to become a person of excellence because you won't have the energy. Bitter resentment will suck your energy away so fast that you won't even be motivated to think about your new dreams, which will leave you stuck living out the same old nightmares.

Impossible Roadblocks Lead to Incredible Success

What about gigantic roadblocks? What about the Mount Everest–sized problems that completely block your path so that it is impossible to get past them to find success? How do you deal with massive problems like breast cancer or divorce? Let me tell you about a friend of mine who had to face an impossible roadblock to get to the incredible success on the other side. Georgia Shaffer is a motivational speaker and author. She is a trainer for the CLASS speaking organization and coaches others on how to become professional speakers. She is sharp, focused, and full of energy, but that was not always the case. She faced a gigantic roadblock and survived. Survival is the goal with gigantic roadblocks, because survival is success. Here is her story.

In the middle of her busy life of parenting and finishing grad school, Georgia noticed a golf ball–sized lump in her breast and immediately had it checked. The surgeon told her it was nothing to worry about, but she insisted on checking it again. Cancer was discovered, and at the age of thirty-eight she had a mastectomy. She had a positive outlook and decided that cancer wouldn't slow her down, yet six months later she had a recurrence. The cancer had aggressively returned, and Georgia was given a 20 percent chance of survival.

Georgia started chemotherapy and then had experimental bone marrow transplants, which nearly killed her. When Georgia was wheeled off the airplane on her way home to recover, she was shocked to learn that her situation was going to get worse. Her husband was divorcing her and had decided to marry another woman. Now she was a single parent with limited disability income and only a slight chance that she would even survive. The next few years of her life were spent fighting insurance companies, fighting divorce, and fighting to stay alive. Her world was overwhelming. Some days she was too weak even to walk to the mailbox. She embraced the personal philosophy of Robert Schuller, who said, "Tough times never last, but tough people do."

Georgia's primary reason for living was her eight-year-old son; she wanted to stay alive to see him graduate. In spite of the cancer, she read to him every night. She described her ability to press on: "The love that friends and family show you and the care they give you keep you going. These people cared if I lived. They were concerned even though I could sometimes see fear in their eyes; they would cry and struggle along with me." Georgia's support system of healthy relationships was an essential part of her recovery. She had built good friendships and invested in other people for years, and they were there to help her during the many years of recovery. By God's grace she survived.

Survive or Thrive?

I asked Georgia to define success. "All the above," she said. "At first it was to see my son graduate. Then success was to live ten years. Success was to pay the bills and keep the house. Success was being paid to speak and write and getting a book contract. Success keeps moving up." Georgia Shaffer shares her story of overcoming impossible roadblocks on platforms across America, including the Crystal Cathedral. She has inspired thousands of people with her books and positive message of moving from a crisis situation, where survival was the only goal, to the next level of success—to thrive. Thriving in spite of the painful problems and roadblocks from the past is to live out the X in the success formula. It is what a success seeker does.

Are you ready to press on to reach for a new destination? Then grab the rope as we climb together to reach for the summit of success.

TWELVE

SUCCESS SEEKERS KEEP CLIMBING

Two roads diverged in a yellow wood,
And sorry I could not travel both. . . .

I took the one less traveled by,
And that has made all the difference.

—Robert Frost

The Chicken Soup for the Soul series of books has been an international phenomenon, with over 70 million copies in print. I asked Mark Victor Hansen, one of the coauthors, to explain the incredible success of this series. He explained it with this powerful statement: "A story can change anyone's life." This collection of wonderful stories has empowered millions of people to face life in a new way. A story has power, and since we are in the final part of our journey together, it is time to let the power of a story change your life. Stories help you to identify the elements of your greatest destination—success! Listen to this true story and learn the lesson of becoming a success seeker.

Two Types of People—Two Different Legacies

Over a century ago, people moved to the midwestern section of the United States to build the greatest agricultural system the world has ever known. These people were called "settlers" because they settled on the fertile land on the western side of the Mississippi River and developed it into productive farms, then into towns, and eventually into states like Kansas, Missouri, Nebraska, the Dakotas, and Iowa. Another group of people, labeled "pioneers," moved farther west to the Pacific Ocean. This group was driven by their hopes and dreams of building their own towns on the other side of the massive Rocky Mountains.

Now, before you jump to the conclusion that one group was more successful than the other, think again. Remember, our definition of success is a balanced view of things that are meaningful and valuable. Someone had to develop and build Kansas. Someone else had the vision to reach the Pacific coast so that more settlers could come to develop and build California. They had to cross the snow-capped Rockies and get beyond the dangers of monster-sized grizzly bears and mountain lions. Add to that the hazard of risking their lives by crossing into unfriendly American Indian territories. They had to deal with bandits along the way without any security or backup from the U.S. Army or the local sheriff.

They also had to contend with the massive challenges of arid deserts, deep river gorges, and climates they had never seen before.

- Why risk everything to go to a place they had never been before?
- What would they do if they lost their way?
- Where would they find clean water?
- How would they survive the cold winters?
- Who would help them if they were under attack?
- What if they lost part of their family along the way?
- Where would they bury a spouse or child with honor, since it was unlikely that they would ever be back that way again?
- When would they finally find a place to call "home" and settle down?

The pioneers had to move beyond their concerns for comfort, stability, safety, and sometimes even common sense. Who in their right mind would liquidate their "safe" life in the city to load their family into a six-foot wooden, horse-drawn wagon to face all of the dangers of life in the West? The pioneers, that's who! Someone had to develop America, so a group of men, women, and children kept pressing on. In 1842 the first wagon train traveled on what would be called the Oregon Trail, which stretched more than two thousand miles across the Great Plains, over the Rocky Mountains, and across the Columbia River. Mountain man Jim Clyman spent his lifetime guiding and protecting the pioneers from innumerable dangers. He said of them, "The long tiresome trip from the States has taught them what they are capable of performing and enduring."

Pioneers proved to themselves and to the world that they could face incredible hardships as they traveled the trail to the Pacific. And that road was eventually littered with broken and useless possessions cast off from thirty years of wagon trains full of dreams heading toward a new life. The trailside was also marked with thousands of graves of loved ones. Perhaps the success of people in the Northwest today is rooted in their pioneer heritage. Their great-great-grandparents developed the real estate, and this new generation developed services and products to impact the world. From Silicon Valley to Starbucks, these Western pioneers have continued to move forward to a place where "no man has gone before." One of the challenges for pioneers is knowing when to stop exploring and start developing the potential of newfound opportunities.

The settler and pioneer principles hold true for you and me. In parts of your life, you may be a settler, and a comfortable one. That's okay for a season. However, at some time you need to move beyond that comfort zone by adding a passion to develop the other parts of your life. Settlers need to work on the different aspects of success to experience growth and eventual stability in those areas as well. True settlers have to face their fear of "Is that all there is?" and move forward to get even more production from an already successful operation. They have to combat the tendency to self-destruct in a certain area of life by setting a new goal of protecting the progress and growth of that area.

Settlers worked hard. They still do. To plant, water, fertilize, and harvest just a little bit more than last year is a great challenge. Settlers maximized the potential of their land. They worked it hard. The results have fed the world. While other parts of the world may have more fertile soil or more favorable temperatures, the settlers produce more crops per square foot than anyone anywhere. They maximize their potential. If you have a chance to drive through the Midwest, you will see the innovations of people who are developing the dream that was handed them by their ancestors. Settlers take what they have been given and maximize it to a new level of success.

Identifying Success for Settlers and Pioneers

In many ways you and I are like the settlers. We have been handed a lifestyle from our family of origin. It includes a genetic health history that we have been given the responsibility to manage. Therefore, we must pay attention to advances in diet, fitness, and healthcare. Settlers take action to insure that their latter years are healthy instead of spent in bed because of poor health choices. We have also been handed educational opportunities, a financial lifestyle, and a personal belief system of work ethics and family relationships. We can comfortably accept those things and never challenge the status quo of the life we were given, or we can act like a true settler and work to reach our potential in each area of life.

Settlers develop and build things that are productive and profitable. Facing your potential and measuring your performance will be a challenge, but you can do it. You can draw out your strengths while moving beyond the limitations of your weaknesses. Insist on maximum results as you actively face your self-imposed limitations.

Pioneers, on the other hand, had very different fears based on the monumental obstacles they faced. The most obvious was the immediate danger of the unsettled wilderness. They had hidden dangers around every turn in the road. Their theme song must have been "Staying Alive!" The one thing that must have given them the strength and courage to move on was the vision of what others had said about the Pacific coast—the big and beautiful ocean, the fertile lands, the massive forests, the abundant game. The promise of great resources and opportunity drew many people. The potential to do more and go places others had never been before drew others. Pioneers are visionaries. They move in new directions and march to the beat of a different drummer. They explore new lands that one day will be occupied by the settlers. They face dangers and conquer obstacles. They press on in spite of any circumstance. Amazing!

You have been a pioneer many times. When you left the safety of your parents and went to your first kindergarten class, you were blazing a new trail. And you were doing the same thing when you moved away from home to go off to college or the military. You definitely were thinking like an adventure-starved pioneer if you got married! That is uncharted territory for anyone! Life threw you many challenges, and you had to face your fears and press on. Life tested your strength of character and your will to survive. You found the courage to move forward in a new way and move beyond your fears. You were like a pioneer discovering new lands. You kept going. You saw the big and beautiful life that awaited you in different places; you "went for it," and you won!

The pioneering spirit in you is why you picked up this book and have begun to rethink and eventually reshape your life into a more successful one. This spirit will keep you going as you think about the difficulties of your past, the people who have hurt you, financial challenges, and problems that stand in the way of your dreams. You may be pressing well beyond what anyone in your family has ever done. Maybe you are the first person in your family to finish high school or college. Maybe you set the standard, without even realizing it, for others to settle behind you. You were building success every time you made a healthy choice to move in a new direction.

Growing into a Success Seeker

Movement is one way to identify success seekers. They live out their dreams and move forward with enthusiasm and joy. As a success seeker, you rewrite your script every time you move beyond your fears to go toward your new destination of a successful life. When you maximize your potential, you create a powerful new story that gets stronger each time you choose to talk, eat, breathe, and function as the successful individual you were designed to become. Augustine must have had the same thought when he said, "Keep adding, keep walking, keep advancing; do not stop, do not turn back, do not turn from the straight road." His challenge was to stop talking about a better life and start moving toward it.

I heard about a couple who were preparing for a yard sale. They were getting rid of a lot of useless junk, including a mirror they had received as a wedding gift. Because of its garish aqua-colored metal frame, they just couldn't find a room in their house where it looked good. Shortly after the yard sale began, a young man looking to decorate his apartment bought it for one dollar. "This is a great deal," he said excitedly. "It still has the plastic on it!" Then he peeled off the aqua-colored protective covering to reveal a beautiful gold-finished frame. The astonished couple had never taken the time to unwrap the covering to discover the beauty underneath.

Success seekers are people who help you to unwrap your gifts and abilities. They can see your potential even when you can't, and they actively go about helping you find success. They are the guides, mentors, and leaders who gain insight by looking into the mirror of their own soul and then sharing those insights with others. They keep growing, so you may have to start climbing to find them at first, but know that it is worth the effort. A success seeker will always help you to find and then live your potential—and even grow into a success seeker for others!

Can Others Steal Your Success?

In turn, as you live out your dreams, it will be your joy to share what you have discovered with others. Don't worry about sharing the secrets of success for fear that people will "steal the good stuff" and leave you in the dust. Your goal is to become your personal best, not to surpass your coworkers or siblings. Besides, if you are climbing toward a new level of success, your fellow climbers will help you, not hurt you. Success seekers are moving toward positive goals and will help you achieve your goals, not toss you aside. They aren't like the woman who raced home, screeched into the driveway, ran into the house, slammed the door, and shouted at the top of her lungs, "Honey, pack your bags; I won the lottery!" Her husband said, "Wonderful! What should I pack—beach stuff or mountain stuff?" She yelled back, "It doesn't matter what you pack; just get the heck out!"

The people who would "throw you under the bus" are in the back of the pack. They are losers who exist by lying, stealing, and cheating to look like they are successful. These people will not make it to the destination of lasting success because they don't have the personal integrity to deal with their own evil behavior. Life will pay them back with some harsh consequences, and they will become miserable failures. Don't waste time with people who are trying to crush your dreams. Just move on.

As you keep climbing toward the person you were meant to become, people will come along to guide you to new places. Success seekers spend their energy pursuing their dreams, not living in the shadow of their old insecurities. As you live out a life of personal excellence resulting from the secrets you have learned on our journey together, you won't have to live in fear anymore. You will be living in the faith that accompanies great people. You will become the type of person who is not afraid to push toward potential regardless of difficult circumstances.

Joseph from the Old Testament was like that. You may have read the story in the Bible of how this young man was sold into slavery by his stepbrothers and eventually was thrown in prison over a false sexual harassment charge. Joe could have become quite bitter; he had every right to be ticked off at the world. Instead, he modeled the attributes of a success seeker. His lifestyle was motivated by his belief that God was in control. This gave him incredible power to perform at his best, because he knew that God blesses based on personal choice in spite of other people's manipulation. Listen to this commentary on his life in prison. "The warden paid no attention to anything under Joseph's care, because the LORD was with Joseph and gave him success in whatever he did" (Gen. 39:23). Joseph would one day become the prime minister of the most powerful culture of his day by living like a success seeker. He kept climbing.

It is time to ask the following important questions about lasting success.

How valuable is your life?

Do you enjoy life or just endure it?

Are you spending your time wisely, knowing you don't get a second chance?

Do you have a specific plan for your present and future success?

Are you working that plan as a life mission?

Are you sharing the success you have discovered with others?

Are you living like a success seeker?

You are responsible for your life and will experience success or failure based on your choices. Success seekers invest their time, relationships, energy, and money doing valuable things that really matter. Even if you can't see a tangible degree of success, you know it's there. Each step you take toward a better way of life is building a momentum of confidence into your soul. Daily disciplines are essential to lasting success. John Maxwell gives this practical advice: "Every day that you are doing the right thing, you are being a success; it just hasn't shown up yet. It's just a matter of time. Success is a process. The secret is discovered in your daily agenda."

Lifelong Learning Is Essential to Success

Teachers often aren't recognized or praised, but they touch your life forever. You have benefited from many education pioneers. One spirited pioneer with a passion for learning was Eddie T. Cromartie Jackson. In 1924 she founded the Booker T. Washington Library in Orlando. She modeled success when she said, "A person cannot travel everywhere, meet people of all types, converse with men of all minds, unless he reads." She made thirty dollars a month working as a school teacher during the day and managed the branch library after school and on weekends. People of color were not allowed in city libraries back then, and she was a visionary about building a place of learning for any person with a desire to grow. During the first six weeks the library was open, hundreds of people registered for library cards, and within a few years the number climbed into the thousands. She took people on the adventure of reading, which is a lifetime habit of success seekers.

Another lifelong success seeker was Bertha Valentine, a public schoolteacher for more than forty years. She faced the poverty of the Great Depression, the sudden loss of her husband early in their marriage to a coal-mining accident, and then the difficulty of being a single mother to two young girls during a time when there weren't many financial resources or programs available to help out single moms. She pursued a summer graduate program and finally obtained a master's degree from the University of Kentucky.

Mrs. Valentine believed that readers would end up being leaders, so she took impoverished mountain children into her one-room schoolhouse and showed them how they could find new destinations of success through books. She touched generations of young people in southeastern Kentucky by teaching them the basics of reading, writing, and arithmetic. She was a pioneer in the preschool educational Head-Start program of helping impoverished kids from one of the poorest parts of Appalachia learn how to read. She knew that a quality education was the only way out of poverty for these children. She bravely faced the stress of parenting alone with the added pressure of having to pay the bills and keep both of her girls focused toward a healthy Christian way of living. She displayed a strong spirit in spite of her obstacles.

Daniel Boone Successfully Opened the Passage

Bertha Valentine's lifetime home was just a few hundred feet from the famed Wilderness Trail that explorer Daniel Boone carved out through the wilderness of Kentucky in the 1700s. Boone was looking for new territory and a safe roadway for wagons to go through what the American Indians called the "Dark and Bloody Ground" because of the many conflicts between warring Indian tribes over Kentucky. Boone successfully took a group of several hundred settlers from the Yadkin River area of North Carolina through a natural gap in the Appalachian Mountains. That area today is known as the Cumberland Gap in the tri-state area where Kentucky, Tennessee, and Virginia meet. The Wilderness Road opened up a passage for settlers moving west for the next hundred years.

I know about that road because Bertha Valentine told me many stories about it. She was a success seeker, and she was my grandmother. She would tell how Daniel and his men built a passage through the mountains along the Cumberland River with primitive tools. No one had ever envisioned it before Boone saw it, then challenged others with his dream. These adventurers partnered together to accomplish the impossible! Boone opened up a passage to get to the Midwest, including Missouri, where he would one day die. He died like he lived, as a pioneer. He had opened up a road to a new place. That's what pioneers do best. I believe God stirs up some people to have what Daniel Boone called "itchy feet," a desire to keep exploring. Others, who follow the great adventurers like Boone, are the settlers who will develop the newly discovered lands. We need both.

My grandmother and I had many wonderful conversations, but I missed out on learning more about the pioneer part of her personality—the part that balanced being a single parent while managing a career. I wish we had talked more about how she "settled" her children. She was a pioneer to me. I was born just a few feet from that same Wilderness Road in the small Kentucky town of Pineville. Throughout my childhood, I heard the stories of Daniel Boone's bravery in facing fears to successfully making it to the other side. As a child, I wore a coonskin cap and had grand adventures with my sister Trish in the big tree in the front yard. We acted out the stories during our childhood playtime, and now as adults she and I live the legacy given to us through the power of those stories.

I grew up wanting to be a pioneering man like Daniel Boone. Perhaps that is why I so enjoy partnering with you as a guide to a new destination of success. I enjoy watching someone come alive in their thinking when they can see a new and better place in their life beyond the obstacles. Coaches are like the leaders from the pioneer expeditions. They help you to open up new places in your thinking. Daniel Boone kept people moving through the mud, cold, threat of Indian attacks, battles with wild animals, and all of the harshness of a newly opened "wilderness." How did he do it? He constantly kept the vision of a better place in front of his struggling group of travelers. He told stories of what the new land was like. He spoke of fertile land as far as the eye could see and of plentiful game and fish. He gave people hope that they could have a better way of life. He painted word pictures with a broad brush. When people heard this mountain man's stories, they wanted to go with him. Daniel Boone inspired my ancestors to move beyond their fears to deal with their self-imposed limitations.

What about you? Can you identify some people from your past who have helped you toward your destination of a better future?

Who in Your Life Has Been a Groundbreaking Pioneer?

Have you taken time to identify and thank the people who taught you to face your fears and move forward? These are the people who challenged you in your education or in your physical health, or perhaps they were the ones who broke a generational pattern of alcoholism or drug or sex addiction. They helped you to move beyond what others in your family of origin had done by blazing a trail to a better place for you. Take a minute and write down the names of your personal pioneers.

_____

_____

_____

Who Has Been a Growth-Oriented Settler?

Have you ever taken time to identify and thank the people who helped you maximize your potential? These are the people who helped you take an area of strength and make it stronger. They brought out the best in your game. They helped you troubleshoot small problems to achieve greater results and enhanced productivity. They modeled a healthy way to manage your finances and lifestyle. Take a minute and identify your personal settlers.

_____

_____

_____

If these people are still alive, you should thank them for helping you move beyond your fears and break through your limitations to live a more successful life. Their leadership aided you in making good choices, and you have experienced a better life because of it. They shared the vision of what you could become and then helped you onto a pathway leading to lasting success.

The Family Secret Is Finally Out

Two settlers who have impacted my life are May and Clint Bain, my parents. They have been my best teachers, and I respect them more than you could imagine but for reasons that might surprise you. I asked for their permission to share these very personal details, and they agreed to expose a difficult time with the hopes of encouraging you to press on toward your goals. You see, they made some mistakes early on in life, and some of their high school classmates thought I was one of them.

Pregnant! The word should bring great joy, but for my parents it brought great panic. They were high school students during the "Happy Days" of the 1950s. They met and quickly fell in love. Love can sometimes lead to lust, and they found themselves intensely involved with each other. Marriage was definitely in the plans, after graduation of course, because you must have an education. Remember my grandmother the teacher? Well, can you imagine the shock when she discovered that her teenage daughter was pregnant? Hopes of graduating would be tossed aside in the crisis of what to do about a baby. What should be done? Well, get married of course—that's what you did in the Eisenhower era. The stress and anguish they went through must have been awful, because other family members had their opinion of what to do about these irresponsible teenagers. I suspect that it was painfully difficult for my parents to do what they did next.

They got married and prepared to have a baby. A travel trailer was purchased as their first home. I was born early on an August morning, almost a month ahead of the scheduled date. I always felt loved and wanted by my parents even though my birth was a source of embarrassment to some.

They protected me from that shame and moved to Florida to get away from the small-town gossip and to give me the security of a loving home. Can you imagine what it must have been like to move hundreds of miles from home with a new baby and many expenses yet no high school degree? When you don't have an education, you either give up or you have to grow up. Fortunately, God blessed me with two amazing parents who are lifelong learners. Because they knew that they needed to learn about raising a child, they read books, listened to parenting programs on Christian radio stations, and went to church to find out how to raise me the "right way." They never stopped learning.

I know that my desire for continual learning came through watching them, and I feel blessed to have had teenagers as parents. They read everything about discovering potential in children and taught it to their kids. I have had success seeker behavior modeled since birth. I watched my parents deal with the twists and turns of life together, even when life was harsh to them. They stood strong. They survived. They are my heroes! One of my mother's favorite sayings is, "Life itself can't give you joy unless you really will it. Life gives you time and space, and it's up to you to fill it." I hope that their story helps you to fill your days with the discovery of lasting success in spite of any circumstance.

No Such Thing as the Success Fairy

Speaker Ken Davis uses the term "success fairy" to describe what many people believe about success. They live their lives as if there is a Tinkerbell floating around waiting to make them happy. The following story from Rachel Remen talks about departing from that kind of flawed thinking and finding a new definition of success.

> A medical doctor described one of his cancer patients, a successful businessman, as becoming depressed unless things went a certain way. Success was "having the cookie." If you had the cookie, things were good. If you didn't have the cookie, life was meaningless. Unfortunately, the cookie kept changing. Sometimes it was money, power, or sex. At other times it was a new car, the biggest contract, or a prestigious address. After his cancer diagnosis the business-man figured out, "It's like I stopped learning how to live after I was a kid. When I give my son a cookie, he is happy. If I take the cookie away or it breaks, he is unhappy. But he is two and a half and I am forty-three. It has taken me this long to understand that the cookie will never make me feel successful for long. . . . Having the cookie is not what life is about." . . . For the first time he feels success-ful. "Two years ago, cancer asked me, 'Okay, what is really important?' Well, life is important. Life. Life any way you can have it. Life with the cookie, life without the cookie. Success does not have anything to do with the cookie; it has to do with being alive." He pauses thoughtfully. "I guess life is the cookie."

The Success Mindset

So here is the final insight: Success is a mindset. It is manag-ing your moods and mastering your motivations. Managing your moods requires discipline to control your impulses while keeping a positive attitude no matter what happens.

Mastering your motivations is discovering and harnessing the powerful drives in your soul. It is understanding the reason you were born. It is living a life of meaning, of being on a mission to share success with others. Hebrews 12:1 says, "Let us run with perseverance the race marked out for us." When the sun comes up, a success seeker will be running on a path to a new destination, a place of greater fulfillment than you ever would have known if you had not joined the race.

You have done well to complete your journey, and there is only one more thing to learn about success: You have already arrived at your destination! You arrived because you have been seeking a new level of insight about the things that matter in your life. Every step takes you toward greater success, but remember that you don't lose the good things you have already accomplished. You had success then, and you have greater success right now. You have reached your destination of success every time you can see and feel and smell and hear and taste and touch a better way of life! Success is here with you—right now. It's like the ending scene in the *Wizard of Oz*, when the mighty Oz tells Dorothy that she always had the power to click her heels and go home. Or like the story of the diamond-seeking traveler who searches the entire world only to miss the acres of diamonds in his own backyard. This Indiana Jones adventure that you and I began has resulted in your discovery of the seven keys to unlock the treasure chest of a better life. With these keys you can now have true success as you come to understand the power of these stories as well as of your own story of discovering success every step of your journey through this life. You see, the journey of success is the joy. It's like the wise saying "Yesterday is past, tomorrow is a mystery, today is a gift; that's why they call it the present."

Enjoy the good life you have discovered from arriving at your destination. I'll be looking forward to hearing your success stories, but don't wait for me. Tell the stories again and again to your fellow travelers of how you found success while you celebrate and climb higher!

NOTES

Chapter 1 Secret #1: Defining What Success Means to You

1. Personal interview, 13 February 2002.
2. Personal interview, 13 February 2002.

Chapter 3 Secret #2: Finding Success Every Day

1. "Seven Wonders," http://jerrismunchies.com/carte.htm.

Chapter 6 Secret #3: Building Success by Mastering Yourself

1. If you want to discover more about the Golden Rule Marbles, which are wonderful reminders of Christ's teaching on becoming a servant leader, contact the Samsonite Corporation, Denver, CO 80239.

Chapter 7 Self-Sabotage: The Most Dangerous Part of You

1. *Biography*, February 2002.
2. Ibid.

Chapter 9 Secret #5: Belief—Finding Your Hidden Source of Inner Strength

1. Pat Morley, *A Look in the Mirror* 43, "How to Sense the Presence of God," http://www.maninthemirror.org/alm/alm43.htm.

2. If you haven't experienced the presence of God and would like to learn more about a personal relationship with Jesus Christ, contact Campus Crusade for Christ at 407-826-2000 or visit their website at www.ccci.org.

3. Fast Company, "Go Ahead, Forward This Email!" http://www.fast company.com/invent/invent_feature/email2.html.

Chapter 11 Secret #7: Excellence—Living the Life You've Always Wanted

1. David Ogilvy, *Ogilvy on Advertising* (New York: Crown Publications, 1983), 11–12.

Acknowledgments

Many dear friends challenged me to write this book. Some are people who have believed in the message of encouragement I have shared with audiences and clients for many years. Some likely didn't even know how much their support meant to me, yet I am grateful to them all. This page is to honor a few of the remarkable people who helped bring this project together.

John Maxwell: John is the greatest leader I have ever known. His personal integrity is a reflection of everything he teaches because he is "real" and lives what he believes. To call John my mentor is a great honor, and to call him my friend is a treasure. I am grateful to him for challenging me to write this book about the secrets of success.

Pat Williams of the Orlando Magic: He heard me give the Successful Life Formula in a speech and immediately came up and said, "That message will be a great book!" He was right on target because he has an amazing ability to spot subjects that touch people's lives. He inspired me to write and then coached me along the way.

Brian Peterson from Revell: He has consistently encouraged me as a writer through the years, and it is a joy to know this man of integrity. He took a simple breakfast discussion at RDV Sports to a new level of success by believing and charting the course for this book project from the very first day he heard about it. What an innovative guy!

Hank and Trish Davis: They gave me a platform to speak about success through their monthly Morinda meeting. The B.O.X. formula was actually born at a team-building session in downtown Orlando. I am grateful to them for believing in the message of success and sharing it with others. I am especially grateful for a sister and brother-in-law who bring even deeper meaning to the word *family*.

Robert Stuart, Joe Christiano, John Adams, Walt Larimore, and Charlie Stuart: These men encourage me to live at a higher level of success through personal integrity and shared insight. It is a joy to know each one of them and a great blessing to call them my friends.

Charlie Wetzel: He prayed with me for direction and focus for this project and then became part of the answer to that prayer by providing me with key writing techniques.

Vanan Hampton, Kristi Keaton, and Jean-Ann Keator: They assisted with research and then read and reread the manuscript for clarity. What a gift!

Shirley McDonald, Priscilla Kelly, and Dianne Brown: They helped me with my schedule and with ideas and gave me encouragement to press on to finish the manuscript.

Jane Williams: She tremendously encouraged me along the many months it took to complete this project and has always believed in my desire to communicate truth.

And finally, thanks to my family—Sheila, Heidi, and Garrett. They all were patient with schedule challenges and writing deadlines. They all understood when I said no to attending some fun family events because I needed to work on this book to encourage others. Now, as promised, let's play and play and play!

Dwight Bain empowers and encourages others to find greater success. He has motivated audiences across America for more than twenty years and is a member of the National Speakers Association.

Dwight Bain would enjoy hearing how this book has impacted your life. He invites you to share how you discovered greater success in your personal or professional life or how these principles positively impacted a family or staff member. To share your success story, or for more information on Dwight's speaking and coaching services and products, contact:

The LifeWorks Group
P.O. Box 1512
Winter Park, Florida 32790-1512
(407) 647-3900
www.dwightbain.com